What You Know by Heart

What You Know by Heart

How to Develop Curriculum for Your Writing Workshop

Katie Wood Ray

HEINEMANN
Portsmouth, NH

Heinemann

A division of Reed Elsevier Inc.

361 Hanover Street

Portsmouth, NH 03801–3912

www.heinemann.com

Offices and agents throughout the world

Library of Congress Cataloging-in-Publication Data

Ray, Katie Wood, 1964–

   What you know by heart : how to develop curriculum for your writing workshop / Katie Wood Ray.

       p. cm.

   Includes bibliographical references and index.

   ISBN 0-325-00364-5

   1. English language—Composition and exercises—Study and teaching (Elementary)—Handbooks, manuals, etc.   2. Language arts (Elementary)—Curricula—Handbooks, manuals, etc.   I. Title.

LB1576 .R375 2002

372.62′3—dc21   2002000790

Editor: Lois Bridges
Production: Elizabeth Valway
Cover design direction: Renee LeVerrier
Cover design: Judy Arisman
Cover photo: Andrew Edgar
Interior design: Jenny Jensen Greenleaf
Typesetter: House of Equations, Inc.
Manufacturing: Louise Richardson

Printed in the United States of America on acid-free paper

06 05 04 03   RRD   4 5

This book is for Cora Silvers Brown,
my grandmother.

Contents

Acknowledgments

Sometimes, the things we know by heart are so much a part of who we are that it's hard to say when or where any of them started. It's hard to pinpoint moments. They come to us over so many seasons of time. All I know is that, for me, they had something to do with . . .

The people who loved me first. My family. My community in Central, South Carolina where I grew up. Their consistent love gave me the confidence to make my way in the world.

The teachers who brought me reading and writing and opened my heart to the wonderful promise of a literate life. The teachers who stretched me to become a thinker, a learner, a researcher. The teachers in Pickens County Public Schools and at Central Wesleyan College and Clemson University and The University of South Carolina. My teachers.

The colleagues who've laughed and cried and learned and loved this thing called teaching with me. The colleagues I've had at Seneca Junior High and Edwards Junior High and the Teachers College Reading and Writing Project and Western Carolina University. My colleagues.

The students who've always been there, challenging me to do this thing called teaching as best I can because they've needed that from me. Even more, they've deserved that from me. They've let me be what I needed to be in the classroom and been willing to come along on many wild journeys. Most of them have given and given and given, even when I've asked so much of them. The students I've had at Seneca Junior High and Edwards Junior High and in the New York City Public Schools and at Western Carolina University. Even the students in other people's classrooms and in my summer workshops who've let me teach them for just a week, a day, an hour. My students.

What I know by heart has come from all the years I've spent living and learning alongside all these different people in all these different places. To all of them I owe and offer a heartfelt thanks.

And to Lois Bridges at Heinemann who guided me to write simply and truly about what was deep inside me. Thank you Lois.

And to my husband, Jim Ray, who reminds me daily that what I know by heart is what matters most. Thank you.

Introduction

On a Tuesday morning in my teaching of writing class at the university, I sat down next to Jennifer for a writing conference. Like the other students in my class, Jennifer had been collecting ideas in a writer's notebook for a couple of weeks. "Tell me a little about how your notebook collecting is going," I asked her. The other students were listening in on our conference.

Jennifer was obviously excited as she launched into telling me about it. "I have some entries that are memories, and some that are observations from different places I've taken it, and," she smiled really big here, "I have the beginnings of a couple of stories I just made up that I really like. I've never really written stories like this."

At this point, I named for her what I saw she was doing. I told her she was finding material that was already sort of written inside her, her memories, that she was gathering material from around her and writing it down, her observations, and that she had stuff she was just making up, her stories. "You've got a nice variety of kinds of entries. Any bumps with anything?" I asked.

"Just one," she explained. "With my stories. I have characters and I have something that's happening to them, but I don't have any idea about the settings. I don't know where the characters are."

"Could you give me an example?" I asked. I was curious about whether the scenes even needed specific settings. I considered that this might not even be the "bump" she thought it was.

"Well, I have this one where a girl is waiting for a guy and she's obviously very upset because her arms are crossed and her legs are crossed and her foot is swinging madly. The guy finally arrives late and they have these really cross words. I'm that far with it, but I have no idea where they are."

I responded, "You know writers of fiction say they start lots of different places—some have to have characters, some have to have some kind of scene happening, some have to have a setting to get started and others don't. You're obviously a writer who can get started without having a setting." Jennifer sort of smiled as we identified her as a certain kind of writer.

I suggested, "If you want to just explore options for settings, you might make a list of possible places the couple could be and then play around in your notebook with placing the couple in these different places and see what happens—see which one seems to feel like the right one. And remember, in some pieces of short fiction, setting isn't really an integral part of the story. You can decide whether it even matters if readers know where the couple is or not. Does that sound like something workable to you?" Jennifer nodded and our conference was over. I made a note of my suggestion to her so I could find out later how it had gone.

Later, after a few other conferences, I brought the class back together and we talked about what they had noticed in each of the writing conferences that day. As we talked about Jennifer's conference, my students kept commenting on how I had affirmed her and didn't make her feel badly for not having a setting. "You were so *not* critical," one of my students said. Their central impression of the conference was to note that Jennifer didn't get in trouble with her teacher for starting a story without a setting. "Isn't every story supposed to have a setting?" another of them asked.

I found my students' (who will soon be teachers of writing) response to Jennifer's conference so interesting. As I thought back on the conference, I realized that it was never in any way a conscious thought of mine that I needed to be affirming to Jennifer in this conference. I never once thought that as her teacher I somehow needed to keep her out of trouble or make her feel okay about missing some story mark. My response to Jennifer in this conference was clearly and simply driven by what I know about writing as a *reader* and a *writer*, not as a teacher. Because I read, I know that setting is not always a factor in stories and I know that some writers say they don't start with settings at all. Because I write and keep a notebook myself, I know that a notebook can be used to experiment with different parts of writing.

I have come to realize that in many ways, I don't even think like a teacher in many of my writing conferences. When I shared these ideas with Jennifer, it was really very much writer to writer. As I listen to students talk about what's happening with them in their writing, I am listening as an insider, as someone who does this too. The feeling of affirmation my students sensed in the conference probably came from watching that in action—a writer to writer kind of talk—that they weren't used to seeing in school.

This feeling of "inside-ness" about the teaching of writing is something I've been thinking about for a long time now and is really the genesis for this book. I know that my experiences as a reader and writer directly inform so much of my instruction in writing workshops, and I have also been privileged to watch so many others anchor their teaching of writing in their own experiences as well. However, knowing that reading and writing can inform teaching, and explaining how it happens, are two different matters.

How is it that as teachers we can move from our own experiences with writing to explicit curriculum knowledge we can use in our teaching? How is it that we can move from reading different kinds of texts to explicit curriculum knowledge about how to write those kinds of texts? In the past several years, my students and I have been studying these curricular moves in our own teaching and in the teaching of others. We have worked at becoming more articulate about how it is that we teach writing from our own experiences, and in doing so have become much more explicit in that teaching. Naming a thought process that was mostly internalized has helped us use that process more efficiently in our teaching.

What You Know by Heart: How to Develop Curriculum for Your Writing Workshop is a very focused book. It's just about us, about teachers of writing and how we can use this thought process to turn our experiences with writing and reading into curriculum for our teaching. Just that one topic. Lots of other things have been left out. This book trusts the body of wonderful professional literature to explore other important aspects of the teaching of writing—workshop management and methodology, conferring, assessment, student writing, craft study—and stays focused on following lines of thinking teachers use to move from their own experiences to curriculum.

Part One of *What You Know by Heart,* "Developing the Curriculum of Process," takes a very close look at the lines of thinking we use to find curriculum in our own writing experiences. Because we don't get to witness the writing process in action as professional authors use it, we have to trust in our own experiences to teach us a lot about how it is that finished writing comes to be. We have to *write like teachers of writing,* the idea that anchors this half of the book.

Part Two, "Developing the Curriculum of Products," takes the same lines of thinking and shows how to use them to find curriculum from our everyday reading lives. All we need to know about how to write anything well can be found in our reading, if we develop the teaching eyes to see it. We have to *read like teachers of writing,* in other words. The book ends with a number of helpful appendices that cite texts we can use to show students different writing possibilities.

As the writer of *What You Know by Heart*, I have had to accept that this book may not be for everybody. Thinking about how we think does not always make for particularly easy reading. Beyond that, there are so many demands and expectations placed on us as teachers today that many will feel they just cannot embark on the journey of learning to teach from their own experiences. The investment of time and energy that journey requires is something many are just unable to give.

But I also know from my experiences working with teachers across the country that there are many who do want to think deeply about this kind of curriculum development. Many of you are in study groups during the school year, in summer institutes and graduate courses, and some of you are just feeding your learning lives on your own. Some of you may be involved in teacher training for the first time and want to learn how to let your reading and writing experiences inform your future teaching. *What You Know by Heart* is for all of you. With you in mind, along the way I've inserted little "Thinking it through . . ." boxes that have questions to think about and things to try as you begin developing your own curriculum. Feel free either to use these boxes as you work your way through the book or to read right past them. I decided to include them because I have found them to be helpful ways of thinking as I've worked alongside teachers in developing curriculum from our own experiences as writers and readers.

My greatest hope is that *What You Know by Heart* will help lead you to stronger, more satisfying teaching in your writing workshops as you share with students what you know about writing, by heart.

Write Like a Teacher of Writing

I am sitting in the airport in Charlotte, North Carolina, and I notice a man sitting near me. He is so like most of the other men I see in airports—briefcase, loosened tie, cell phone. He's obviously on his way to or from a business meeting, like hundreds of others in the airport this night. He is so like the men I am used to seeing, except for one thing: he is hunched over a colorful piece of material and his hands are carefully cross-stitching.

Cross-stitching. I stare for awhile. He doesn't notice me; he's intent on his work. I pull out my notebook and I write the entry shown in Figure 1–1.

As soon as I am finished writing the entry and, rereading it, thoughts enter my mind:

This entry is a keeper. I need to share it with my students. It's interesting how, as I was writing it, I was thinking about my thinking. I was almost talking to myself as I wrote it—scolding myself for thinking this. Sort of like writing it at two levels—my thinking and my reaction to my thinking. I need to show this to my students. Hmm . . . this guy would make a great character too . . .

> In the Charlotte Airport, a man sits near me and he is doing cross-stitch! I can't really tell — it may be needlepoint. I am blown away by the sight of it, and of course I know it is my whole gender lens I'm looking through that is making me not believe my eyes. I mean, it's easier for me to believe men would do cross-stitch than it is to believe they would do it sitting in such a PUBLIC place. Seems like it's something he ought to hide. And the thing is, he's such a normal looking guy. Oh, my gosh! This is so <u>biased</u> of me! But it's just so weird to me. Okay — now we've boarded and he's in 1st class. New wonderings... Who is this cross-stitching guy? What <u>should</u> a cross-stitching guy look like?!

FIGURE 1–1 *Notebook Entry*

Why Teachers of Writing Write

We know that writing is something that people do, that it doesn't just happen. Memoirs and feature articles and editorials and poems all come to be because someone, somewhere *does* a whole bunch of stuff. There is so much that happens behind any piece of writing we see that's finished. There is so much *doing* behind it, and in writing workshops today we are asking our students to get very involved in all the things that writers in the world actually do. The problem is, when we were in school, most of us never did the kinds of things we now ask our students to do. If we do not do them as teachers, then, we would actually be trying to teach our students how to do things we've *never* done ourselves.

This is why so many of us try—at least once—the things we are asking students to do in our writing workshops. We live in the world as writers, searching for and capturing ideas for writing (that's what I was doing in the airport). We keep notebooks with these ideas in them. We take some of those ideas and grow them into something bigger that we eventually write for real audiences or for other reasons that matter to us. We draft, revise, and edit those pieces. We share them with others and deal with their feedback in our revision. We write in a variety of genres and forms. We write about the same topics in different ways. We give our writing away to others, finding out how scary that can be, and how joyous. Basically, we try to do for ourselves the things we are going to teach students how to do.

We write so that we know what to teach about how this writing work gets done. We write so that we know what writers think about as they go through the process. We write so that our curriculum knowledge of the process of writing runs deep and true in our teaching. We write so that we can explain it all.

> ### Thinking It Through...
> You might make a list of the kinds of things you ask students to do as writers during the year. As you look at the list, ask yourself, "What parallel experiences do I have to what I ask my students to do?"

Now, we are not alone in our efforts to understand the process of writing. We can call on our co-teachers of writing to explain some of it. We have lots of co-teachers of writing—Cynthia Rylant, Rick Reilly, Jacqueline Woodson, Gary Paulsen. They sit on our bookshelves and in our magazine baskets patiently waiting to show our students and us great writing moves. Sometimes, in interviews and books and articles, these great writers talk a little about what we can't see in their finished pieces of writing. They tell us things about how they get the writing done, and we listen like teachers of writing—and we learn a lot.

When we hear Billie Letts say, "I walked in a Wal-Mart and looked around and I thought, 'You could live here. There's everything you need. You could exist in this place.'" This happening, this walking-into-Wal-Mart, was the beginning that led Letts to write the novel *Where the Heart Is* (1995). So we hear her say this and then we know: *writers get ideas for writing when they are away from their desks. Writers can get ideas at Wal-Mart.* This becomes something we can teach our students.

Or, when we hear Barbara Kingsolver say that the way she worked on *The Poisonwood Bible* was "to spend about a year in writing exercises and I would imagine a scene and then I would write the same scene from five different points of view," we know: *sometimes writing takes a long, long time* and *sometimes writers do exercises before they draft.* These become things we can teach our students.

As teachers of writing, we know a lot about what our co-teachers have to say about how they get their writing done. We build curriculum knowledge from things professional writers have said about the process of writing, and we share all that we possibly can of this with our students who are learning to write. There is so much our students can learn from these people who do what the students are learning to do. As a matter of fact, there is so much to learn from these other writers, that it might seem to trivialize *our* writing. Why should students learn from our experiences with the writing process when they could be learning from Barbara Kingsolver? When there is so much good curriculum available in other writers' "talk," why do we need to write in order to understand what we are teaching?

Because we breathe when we're in classrooms.

We breathe, in and out, and some of us trip over things and have funny hair and great shoes and horrible jokes we can't remember the punch lines for and husbands and wives and pets and because some of us are scared of spiders. You see, we are live people students can see doing what they are trying to do. And we don't have to do it well! There's no pressure for us to do it well because Cynthia Rylant and Gary Paulsen can do it well. We just have to do it and breathe at the same time. We need to be alive in the room with our students as we write. Our students need to see in us what we're hoping for in them, and no other writer can do that for them because we're the only ones breathing in the room with them.

Now, as teachers of writing, we don't need to write a lot or even very often. We can't; we're very busy. In my past, I have tended to do a lot of writing in the summers, sometimes in summer institutes. Once I've done it, I have that experience in my "teaching file" for the rest of my career. I still frequently use writing from notebooks and drafts I did ten years ago, and all along the way since, to develop curriculum for minilessons and conferences.

At different times, we may work very purposefully on some writing so that we can understand it better for our teaching. The first time we take a group of students through a genre study that is new to us, for instance, we can spend time living like a writer of that genre in the world and in our notebooks. We can work like writers of that genre, and we can draft and go public (in some way) with a piece of writing in that genre. But once we have done this, we don't have to do it every time we start a study of that genre with new students. As teachers of writing, we can return again and again to material we've developed in the past for poetry, fiction, persuasive writing, and on and on.

I think it is important that we are up front about *how much* when we discuss teachers of writing and their writing. We don't need to have these incredibly active writing lives to understand the process of writing as insiders, but we do need to have tried, at least once, to do the things we are asking our students to do. And we need these to be *quality* experiences, experiences we have examined deeply enough to know what they teach us about how writing happens.

Looking Closely at Our Writing Experiences

As teachers of writing, we can't *just write*. We have to write so that we come to understand what it is that we are teaching. We have to push ourselves to notice and understand what's happening when we write, so that our writing becomes a powerful curriculum tool for our teaching. If we don't push ourselves to examine our writing in this way, then it can fall flat in our teaching.

Many of us have started our own writer's notebooks and drafted important, meaningful pieces of writing out of those notebooks. Often we have done this as a requirement for a course in the teaching of writing or in a summer writing institute. After engaging as writers ourselves, we return to our classrooms with new energy for the teaching of writing. But over time, that energy starts to fade because we're not sure how to use our writing experiences to generate curriculum for our teaching. We know that we have written. We know that the writing experience was powerful, and we share that with our students. But once we've shared that, we kind of think, "Okay, now what else am I supposed to say about this?" We're left not really knowing what to do with our own writing experiences when we teach.

Again, what I think we have to remember is, we can't *just write*. We are teachers of writing. Danielle Steele can *just write* if she wants. So can Dave Berry and Stephen King and Toni Morrison. They can all *just write* because they are *just writers* (imagine that, accusing Toni Morrison of being "just a writer"). The only thing waiting for them in the future is the next romance novel, feature article, thriller, Nobel prize for literature. Now, those things may be waiting in our futures, too, but that's not all. Our students are waiting in our futures. We are *teachers of writing* and that means we can't *just write*. We have to write like the kind of people we are.

We do everything this way. We move through the world being the kind of people we are. I have a whole different experience in a kitchen store than my friend Rick because I am the kind of person who cooks and he is not. My ears perk up when I hear people talking about airport delays and lost luggage because I am the kind of person who travels. I notice whether the motorcycle passing me is a Honda or a Harley or a Ducati because I am the kind of person who's into motorcycles. And when I write, I write like the kind of person who teaches writing. I write like a teacher of writing. I can't help it. It's who I am.

Because we are teachers of writing, writing for us is more than just the experience of getting it done. We have to have that experience, but because we teach, we also have to be able explain that experience We have to be able to make sense of it, to see what it means so that the experience becomes something larger than the moment. The experience becomes something we understand about writing. It becomes curriculum. You see, the students who wait for us in our workshops need us to help them understand how this writing thing happens. That's why we can't just let it happen. We have to know why it happens. We have to know how. More than publication waits for us at the end of our journey.

I find that experiences like the one in the airport happen to me all the time. From professional writers I have learned to live in the world as a writer. I have learned that people we notice—like the cross-stitching man—can become wonderful characters for fiction, can move us to think in ways that lead us to essays, can become the focal points for poetry. If I am going to support a writing life, I need material like this. I keep a writer's notebook and I "throw in" material like this all the time.

But I also live in the world like a teacher of writing who, when she writes, knows that there is curriculum embedded in the whole process of what she is doing. The thinking that followed my writing of this entry is curriculum thinking. I see a lesson in what happened as I wrote the entry. Using this entry as an example, I could teach students a lesson on how to *talk back to your entry if you are aware of your thinking as you are writing*.

In this case, I certainly didn't set out to write this kind of talking-back-to-my-thinking entry. The me that is a writer was really struck by this man and so, out of habit, I grabbed my notebook and started writing. It just happened that as I was writing, I became aware of how biased my thoughts were, and I embedded that thinking in my entry. It wasn't until I reread the entry that I really noticed how I had written it at two levels. When I noticed this, my very next thought was, *I could show this to my students*. In other words, the curriculum was generated when my teacher-self took a close look at what my writer-self was doing. Lots of our best writing curriculum is generated this way. We simply carry on as writers knowing that if we do, what we need to teach about writing will become clear along the way, if we develop the eyes to see it.

Take, for example, this chapter you are reading right now. So many things happened as I was drafting this chapter and every one of those things is a little story about what happens when someone writes. One of those stories goes like this: Pages and pages of this chapter got moved to another chapter. Originally I was going to put the ideas of "write like a teacher of writing" and "read like a teacher of writing" into the same chapter. I started drafting it this way and in the process realized it was getting too swampy. The ideas were both so big, and they seemed to get bigger the more I drafted. So, while connected in many ways, I decided to separate the ideas and make them the cornerstones for two separate chapters. It was scary to do this. It felt sort of like starting over, and I wasn't sure I had the energy to start over or if it would really work. But I felt I had to try because the draft was just getting too bogged down to work well.

That's what happened. And if I leave it at that, it will be just that: a writing experience that happened. But because I am a teacher of writing, and I know that I work with students who also write drafts that sometimes get swampy, drafts about trips to camp and soccer tournaments and cheerleading, I realize that this is more than an experience, this is curriculum: *if your draft feels like it's got too much going on in it, you might try breaking it up into different sections or even whole different pieces*. I have a story to tell about how this happened to me, and I can explain this option to students by telling them my story. I can also tell them the part about it being scary, about how it feels to take this huge part of a draft and move it somewhere else. I can explain this human side of the process because I've been there.

I think it's important to say that we don't have to be writing something as major as a book to be living on this human side of the writing process. We can engage on a much smaller scale and develop these same kinds of under-standings—a poem for our daughter's birthday, a memoir to share with the family, a picture book for our class library. All we need is a good reason of our own to write something and an audience of at least one person we can give it to when it's finished. That's all we need to experience what it is we are trying to teach our students to do in the writing workshop and to develop important curriculum.

When we use our own writing experiences to de-velop curriculum, there always seem to be these two sides to it. On the one hand there is the strategy side of it, the "what I did that you might try" side of it. But there is also this other, more intimate kind of teaching hap-pening. The human side. We don't just teach the pro-cess; we teach what it is like to be *a writer going through the process*. This is so critical to our teaching.

Thinking It Through... ⟳

In your own teaching, when are students most likely to experience your "human side"? When do your own experiences most influence your teaching? What difference does it make when you teach from your own experience?

You know, we ask our students to give so much of themselves when they write. We ask them to write about things that matter. We ask them to invest enormous amounts of time and energy to write about those things well. And then, the crowning request, we ask them to take their writing out into the world and give it to other people. We need to know how it *feels* to do what we are asking them to do. We need to understand the very human side of what we are teaching when we teach writing.

The Nature of Process Curriculum

As teachers, we know that every encounter we have with writing is essentially an act of curriculum development. Our experiences with writing are essentially experiences with the *process of writing,* the process that leads us on a journey that begins with having an idea and ends with that idea going out to an audience in some finished, written form. As teachers of writing, we ask our students to go on this journey of process again and again and we support them with teaching as they travel.

The curriculum we offer students in this teaching comes from everything we know about *how* someone goes on the journey of process. We are searching, basically, for the answers to two questions:

Thinking It Through…

Before reading on, you might try thinking about what you already know about these questions of process. You might choose a part of the process—say revision—and jot down a list of some things you know writers think about and do as they revise. As you make the list, ask yourself, "How do I know this? Where am I getting this curriculum knowledge?"

What kinds of things do writers think about, and why do they think about these things? (understandings)

What kinds of things do writers do, and how and why do they do them? (strategies)

Let's open those two ideas up just a little now and think about what kinds of things we are trying to learn (so we can teach) as we write like teachers of writing.

Understandings

Recently, in a conference with a second grader, I listened as a young writer explained to me that he had been working for several days on the draft of a story I could see laid out in front of him. "Let me ask you a question," I said. "Do you think about this story when you're away from school? Away from writing workshop? Do you think about it when you're at home or out playing or doing chores with your mom or dad?"

"No," he said. "Not really."

"Hmm . . . " I replied. I had my teaching direction. I opened my notebook and showed this young writer pages in it that were marked with different codes and I explained that these were pages where I put ideas for the writing project I was working on at the time. "I think about it all the time," I told him. "Even when I'm not actually writing it, I'm still thinking about it and talking about it to other people and having ideas for it." I helped him think about how he might live like this for awhile, live like a writer consumed by a project. We imagined him thinking of his story while he was on the playground, talking through ideas with friends and family, dreaming about it at night. Together we envisioned what it might look like if he tried this: *think like a writer when you're away from your writing desk*. We parted with an agreement to talk again in a day or two about how this had gone for him.

The curriculum I offered this young writer during our conference, the *what* of what I taught him (the specific content) is something I know about writing because I have experienced it firsthand. I know that when writers are working on a piece of writing over time, they don't just think about it at the writing desk, they think about it off and on all the time. This is an essential *understanding* I have about writing. Much of the curriculum around the process of writing is a lot like this, and a lot of times it looks and feels so different from more traditional, empirical kinds of curriculum—the steps of mitosis, for instance, or states and capitals.

Sometimes when we teach children *understandings* about writing, the teaching feels not quite solid enough at first. But later, when we see what a difference these understandings can make in students' writing, later when this little second-grade boy comes to school and announces he has some great new ideas for his story because he thought about it all last evening, then we realize the rigor behind the teaching. We have to get comfortable with the fact that students need help understanding how it is a person does this writing work, that they need these understandings just as much as they need to know where apostrophes go or different options for structuring a text or how to write compelling leads.

Because we have been on journeys through the writing process, there are lots of things we understand about how that journey goes. We know what kinds of things a person thinks about when on this journey, and all of these things are important curriculum. Offering students this curriculum helps them develop important understandings about their work as writers and ultimately helps them *do* things better.

We will develop lots of these understandings because we write ourselves, but we can also listen to other writers and be watchful for what we can learn from their understanding about the process. For example, in an interview with Karen Hesse I found on Scholastic's website, this author says of writing, "There are times that the writing goes so well that I feel I have been given a gift. Then there are times it goes so slowly, it feels like torture. But I know that if I stay at the computer—if I keep at it with every word and every image—it will be okay."

When we read this quote like teachers of writing, we find a very important understanding in it: *sometimes you just have to keep at it, even when it feels like torture.* This becomes something we can teach students about the process of writing. When we see writers struggling with how hard writing can be at times, we tell them about Karen Hesse, and we help them come to understand that this is a normal part of the process. This important understanding will help them steer through the waters of "things being hard" and come to the other side.

Strategies

In addition to having a lot of understandings about how someone goes through the process of writing, when we write ourselves we also know what kinds of things a person *does* to get through this journey, and these too become important curriculum in the form of strategies we can suggest. *You might try listing all the parts you want to include; or, you could take an entry and try asking questions about it just to get your thinking going; or, get someone else to read it, tell it back to you, and then listen to see if it made sense.* We try things as writers as we engage in the journey of this process, and these things we do can become things we might suggest another writer try. The nature of this kind of curriculum is strategic.

Students need to know what kinds of things writers do, throughout the process, to get their writing done. They need to know strategies for getting ideas; growing ideas; and drafting, revising, and editing those ideas for publication. As teachers of writing, we pay very close attention to exactly what it is we are doing as we write, how we are doing it, and why we are doing it. We have to pay attention so that we can teach students—in a strategic way—how to do these same things.

We also pay attention when our co-teachers of writing talk about going through this process. We listen for the action verbs in what they say. We need to know what they do because, whatever it is, it becomes something our students might do as well. For example, in that same interview with Karen Hesse on Scholastic's website, we learn that Karen often looks at a photograph of someone as she is writing, that this helps her develop realistic characters. This becomes something we might suggest that students try when writing fiction: *try finding a photograph of someone to represent your character and keep that photo with you as you write your character's story* (just like Karen Hesse does). This becomes a piece of *strategic* curriculum.

Layers and layers of understandings and strategies make up the curriculum of process. As teachers of writing, we have to know how to turn our experiences with writing into this kind of writing curriculum. We have to live with a very real sense of the future, knowing that students wait for us at the end of our writing process. They will want to know, "How was it? Did it go okay?

Thinking It Through...

What do your students already know about you as a writer? Do they see you as being like them (someone who writes) in that way?

What can you tell me about the ride?" We represent, in living, breathing form, a person who has "been there and done that" when it comes to writing. When we get together in summer writing institutes and courses on writing, I think we need tee shirts that say, "My teacher went to writing camp and all I got was this great curriculum."

References

Hesse, Karen. "Authors and Books–Author Studies–Karen Hesse–Interview Transcript." Retrieved from www.scholastic.com

Kingsolver, Barbara. "Oprah's Book Club–Writers on Writing–The Preparations." Retrieved from www.oprah.com

Letts, Billie. "Oprah's Book Club–Writers on Writing–Sources of Inspiration." Retrieved from www.oprah.com

———. 1995. *Where the Heart Is*. New York: Warner.

CHAPTER 2

From Writing to Writing Curriculum

Once upon a Time When I Was Writing . . .

When we think about how to generate curriculum from our own writing experiences, it helps to think of those experiences as actual *texts*, little narrative stories with beginnings, middles, and ends. Every writing experience is a little story of someone writing. We can then read these stories in much the same way that we read a book or a letter or a newspaper article. We can think back on what has happened (an experience) and search its meaning (read it).

If we only take the time to read the stories of our experiences, there are layers and layers of meaning around most everything that happens in our lives—phone calls, shopping trips, what we're cooking for dinner. There is never just the thing that happens, there is always the whole world, the whole life in which it happens as well. Now, we don't have the time to read that deeply into most of what happens in a day, but that doesn't mean the smallest moments aren't rich with meaning. As teachers of writing, we spend time reading the texts of our experiences as writers because the curriculum of *process* (how it *happens* that someone gets writing work done) is folded into the layers of meaning in these texts.

You see, every time we write, we are actually creating two texts. One is an actual, tangible text—a notebook entry, a draft, a revision scratched in the margin, and one is a living text, a text of a lived-through experience. When we read them together, these two simultaneously written texts become our main curriculum guide for teaching the process of writing.

To read this curriculum guide on process, we can use a line of thinking very similar to the one many of us use to study the craft of writing (Ray 1999, 120). Note the similarity:

Craft Study Thinking	Process Study Thinking
NOTICE something in the text.	NOTICE (or look at) something you have done or thought about as a writer.
TALK ABOUT IT and MAKE A THEORY about why the writer might have crafted it this way.	DESCRIBE what you have done or thought about, and why you did it or thought about it.
NAME what it is, exactly, the writer is doing in the text.	NAME, in some generalized way, what you did or thought about.
CONNECT IT, if you can, to another text you know in which a writer is doing the same thing.	CONNECT what you have done or thought about, if you can, to another writer's process.
ENVISION yourself or your students making this same craft move in your writing.	ENVISION your students doing this or thinking this as they write.

When studying the craft of writing, we use this line of thinking to see how a text is written; not what it's about, but how it's written. We are looking to see how the text is structured, how words and sentences and paragraphs are used, how specific genre elements are developed. We are reading actual texts—newspaper articles, picture books, novels, poems—when we are studying the craft of writing in this way. Essentially, studying the craft of writing is a study of the *product* itself, the actual text that is created. We will use this line of thinking later in the book as we explore what it means to *read* like a teacher of writing.

When studying the *process* of writing, we read in much the same way—to see how it is done—but instead we are reading the text of the *experience* of writing. We look at the texts of our experiences to see where ideas come from, how those ideas are developed, how a writer gets a draft started, what happens along the way as the draft progresses, and on and on. We read the texts of our experiences as writers so that we can become articulate about how writing *happens*, articulate about the curriculum of writing process. We return over and over to those two questions we outlined in the last chapter: What kinds of things do writers do, and how do they do them? And, what kinds of things do writers think about, and why do they think about these things?

When teachers of writing study either the craft of writing or the process of writing we are singular in our purpose: curriculum development. We need to know, *by heart*, what it is we are trying to teach when we teach writing. The "end of the line" for our thinking is always the same: what can we now envision, either for texts or for process, that could happen in our students' work? The visions we are left with become curriculum possibilities for our teaching. Internalizing this line of thinking that we can use for both process study and craft study (products) is critical if we are to write and read like teachers of writing.

Process Study Thinking

By reading the "texts" of our writing experiences as stories, we can use this line of process study thinking to develop writing curriculum. To demonstrate this way of thinking, I'll take a personal writing experience and show how to move from a writing experience to writing curriculum. I am going to do it fairly exhaustively just to show *how much* potential there is an a single experience. I want to make it clear that we don't have to have lots of writing experiences to have lots of writing curriculum. We just need to read the experiences we do have more deeply. And please remember that I am trying to get thinking down on paper here, so it might look fairly complex spelled out like this. Once we learn to think in this way though, moving from writing to writing curriculum will become a habit of mind that is fairly easy to use.

NOTICE (or look at) something you have done or thought about as a writer

Looking back through an old notebook, I come across an entry that catches my attention. I remember well the afternoon I wrote the entry. I am struck by it for several reasons, the most prominent one is the feeling of remorse that I've never pursued the entry further. I try and let that go, however, and I realize the experience behind the entry is one that is probably rich with curriculum, rich with things to know about how one lives as a writer. I decide to "read this experience" to see what it teaches about writing.

DESCRIBE what you have done or thought about, and why you did it or thought about it

Here is where I tell my story, my "once upon a time when I was writing" story. Notice that I actually think of it as a story, beginning, middle, and end:

> One late September a few years ago I was riding on the back of my husband's motorcycle through the Great Smoky Mountains where we live. It was a glorious early fall day and as we were riding, I was noticing how the changing leaf colors start at the tops of the mountains (where it's coldest) and work their way down. I was thinking about how this is the opposite of spring when the trees start "greening" from the bottoms of mountains (where it's warmest) and work their way up to the top. As I was

thinking about this, a title came to me: *When Autumn Comes Down the Mountain*. It sounded like the title of one of those picture books I love so much, one that dances around with language to describe some beautiful thing in nature. A book like *Water Dance*, by Thomas Locker or *The Whales* by Cynthia Rylant. A book like I've always wanted to write.

As we continued to ride along, I began to make up lines and phrases in my head for this book *When Autumn Comes Down the Mountain*. I would say them out loud just to see how they sounded (I wear a full-faced helmet so no one knows I am just talking away to myself). I thought of lines like this: "At first it's just a whisper, a blush." And lines like this: "A summer mountain is heavy with green." They just kept coming to me as we sped along, and before long I was getting anxious. I needed my notebook and I needed us to stop so I could write some of the lines down before I lost them. I just kept repeating the lines I liked over and over so I wouldn't forget them. As I repeated them, I would say them in different ways, taking words in and out, moving words around, imagining how I might punctuate them to get them to sound different ways.

When we finally did stop, I went straight for my notebook and started writing. I knew I needed to write fast and get down everything I could remember, so I forced myself to just write lines down as a list rather than trying to draft the picture book right there on the spot. That was a little hard for me because I was so excited and wanted it to read like a beautiful picture book right away. But I did it; I made myself just write lines down. Once I started, more came to me. Figure 2–1 shows the list of lines I made in my notebook.

When I felt I had generated all the lines I could, I stopped, happy that I had gotten them down and satisfied that I could return to the list of lines someday and actually try and shape them into a draft of a picture book text, *When Autumn Comes Down the Mountain*.

Thinking It Through...

Before reading on, you might want to think about a time when you were really working on some writing. Try and remember something you thought about or something you did while writing. It might be something as small as a simple revision or an idea for a draft. Just make sure it's something specific. On some paper or in a conversation, begin with "Once upon a time when I was writing . . ." and then write or tell, in as much detail as possible, about what you thought about or what you did. The key is to try and get comfortable with thinking of your writing experiences as little stories.

* When autumn comes down the mountain *

* At first, it's just a whisper, a blush.
when it starts ⟋ → It begins as just...

* Autumn ~~comes~~ spreads flat in the wideness of the lowlands

* You see it beat around the edges of the day,
When the light is right and the air is
clear with the going and coming of night.

* You always feel a change in the air
first, a coolness that makes you look
up to the tops of mountains

* like a slow syrup of color poured over
the top that slowly reaches for the
~~bottom~~ valley

* There is gold and red and orange and,
here and there, a hanging-on green

* ~~All~~ As autumn begins it's slow journey
to the valley

* A mountain in winter is blue and gray
quiet. A winter mountain waits, quiet
and gray, and ~~stilled~~ grown still ~~to~~ with the cold.

* Waits for when it can draw up the warm
green ~~from~~ the valley, draw it slowly
to the top.

* A summer mountain is heavy with green,
draped in green, made from green.

* You think ~~there~~ must be just this green—
no brown earth or blue sky above ~~because~~
the green is so ⟨velvet overpowering⟩ ?

* slow like syrup it moves

* Before long, everything starts to rustle...

* time in between seasons/writing time

* We are always moving toward the next
season

FIGURE 2–1 *Notebook Entry*

NAME, in some generalized way, what you did or thought about

As I look closely at the story of this experience, as I read it as text, I see that there are several layers of things to know about writing in this one story, several understandings and strategies we can name specifically. Any one of these (by itself, or in some combination) could become the content of a minilesson or a writing conference with a student. Let's consider the understandings and strategies as they appear in the description of my writing experience that you just read. As we name them, notice how one leads to the next in a kind of seamless progression of process. Notice also that each curriculum statement has been untied from my writing story and generalized. I'll write the curriculum statements in italics so they are clear.

The first is an important understanding, one I know well as a writer: *sometimes writers get their best ideas far away from the desk.* I was about as far away from my writing desk as I could have been when I had this idea for writing. I wasn't trying to think of writing ideas at all. I was simply enjoying time with my husband and the beauty of the mountains in fall. But because writing is something I do regularly, things that strike me often strike me as ideas for writing. Any number of people riding through the mountains on that September day would have been struck by the leaves beginning to show their colors, but because I am a writer it struck me as a writing idea too.

Another related yet separate understanding is how the idea actually came to me: *sometimes ideas come to you in the form of perfect titles.* Most ideas don't come to me this way, but in this case there was really something about thinking of that title, *When Autumn Comes Down the Mountain,* that got me excited about the idea. The best way I know how to explain it is that it was like dreaming of names for your children. It felt sort of like that. Having the title helped me imagine writing this and all that it could be.

Related to the idea coming to me as a title is another important understanding about writing: *sometimes the form writing should take is apparent right from the start.* I knew right away that this was the title of a picture book, that this was the form of writing that would make the most sense for the kind of writing I was dreaming of making. I even knew the kind of picture book it would be—thinking of specific touchstone texts almost immediately. Many of the writing ideas I collect kind of randomly in my notebook don't come to me this way at all. When I first find them, I have no specific vision for what I'll do with lots of the ideas I put in my notebooks. I just know I need ideas so I throw them in there.

I really believe in this case, seeing the idea from the start as a picture book with a title is what led me to actually start composing lines for it there on the back of that motorcycle. So this actually leads me to another important understanding: *sometimes knowing the form your writing will take leads you to precise language.* I have the sound of language in books like *Water Dance* (Locker 1997) and *The Whales* (Rylant 1996) embedded deep inside me because I have read them so many times. As soon as I knew that I was thinking of writing that would have this sound, then, I was able to think in terms of very specific language.

Now for a strategy I see in the text of my experience: *try composing lines out loud (in different ways) to see how they sound.* This is something a writer can do anytime, anywhere. Because I lived through this experience, I know that it was important for me to say the lines out loud, rather than just think them. This is probably related to the picture book form again; I was imagining writing that would be read aloud so I wanted to hear how it sounded out loud.

On the heels of this strategy is another understanding: *sometimes you can see different potentials for revision and punctuation by reading lines out loud in different ways.* The experience with this was so interesting to me. As I played with the line, "At first it's just a whisper, a blush" I kept thinking of different ways I could write it. I thought about how it would sound with a comma after the first two words, "At first, it's just a whisper, a blush." I wondered if I should repeat "just" so it read, "At first it's just a whisper, just a blush." I tried putting "blush" first, "At first it's just a blush, a whisper." And several other combinations, each said out loud until one sounded just right and I could see how it would go down on the page.

Another strategy, a simple one, but one that really mattered to me that day as a writer is this: *if you think of something good, keep repeating it so you won't lose it before you can get to some paper to write it down.* I was caught in a situation where the physical act of writing was impossible and I was having all this great stuff come to me. As soon as I realized that I was on to some good stuff, I just tried to stay focused and kept repeating the lines I liked over and over. I had them memorized by the time I got to my notebook, but more importantly, I didn't lose them. There is nothing sadder to a writer than to have had some great words and have lost them (that's an understanding, but that's also another story).

When I finally got to my notebook, I had to employ another strategy: *try making a list if you are trying to get a lot of separate ideas down fast. You can figure out how they go together later.* This was actually an important strategy for me to make myself use. I *really* wanted to sit down and just draft this picture book I had dreamed up so it would start, right away, to look and feel like I dreamed it could be. But because I know myself and my drafting process, I knew it would go very slowly as I would labor over every single word (like I always do) and then I would lose some of this good stuff I had composed in my head. So I forced myself to just get it down. Wrapped inside my decision to make this writing move (making the list) is actually another fairly sophisticated under-standing: *sometimes what we know about ourselves as writers can help us decide the best way to proceed with our work.*

So we'll stop there. I can imagine there may be even more as yet uncovered layers of meaning in this writing experience, but that's what I see in it with a first reading. Let's list all the "chunks" of curriculum so we can see them in one place, untied from the discussion around them. And remember, these are nine separate things I can now teach about writing.

Understandings

◆ Sometimes writers get their best ideas far away from the desk.

◆ Sometimes ideas come to you in the form of perfect titles.

◆ Sometimes the form writing should take is apparent right from the start.

◆ Sometimes knowing the form your writing will take leads you to precise language.

◆ Sometimes you can see different potentials for revision and punctuation by reading lines out loud in different ways.

◆ Sometimes what we know about ourselves as writers can help us decide the best way to proceed with our work.

Strategies

◆ Try composing lines out loud (in different ways) to see how they sound.

◆ If you think of something good, keep repeating it so you won't lose it before you can get to some paper to write it down.

◆ Try making a list if you are trying to get a lot of separate ideas down fast. You can figure out how they go together later.

CONNECT what you have done or thought about, if you can, to another writer's process

When other writers talk about the process of writing, I always listen very closely. These other writers might be professional ones speaking in interviews or writing in books about writing, or they might be my students talking about their own processes. I am listening for strategies and understandings that match my own, and for ones that are quite different from my own. Both kinds of connections help me to deepen what I know about the process of writing. There is never just one understanding to have about something in writing, never just one strategy that gets us where we need to go.

To show how making connections works in process study thinking, let's look at just a few of the curriculum chunks in my writing experience and make some connections. Take the first understanding: *sometimes writers get their best ideas far away from the desk.* There are so many other writers who have said this that you almost think this one could be chalked up as gospel. Billie Letts, as we mentioned in the last chapter, walked into a Wal-Mart and got the idea for *Where the Heart Is* (1995). Lee Smith, another one of my favorite writers, also gets ideas while shopping: "I went to the outlet mall in Burlington and nobody would wait on me in Linens-n-Things because they had this book, and they were all in there interpreting each other's dreams. It was hysterical. So I came home and wrote the story, 'The Interpretation of Dreams' right then, that weekend" (Powell 1995, 399).

Connections like these are so important because each one takes this essential understanding—*sometimes writers get their best ideas far away from the desk*—and gives it a new living story, a whole new context different from my own. In my teaching, when I share connections like these they help students see that it's not about being on the back of a fast motorcycle in the mountains in North Carolina and having ideas. You could be in Linens-n-Things. In Wal-Mart.

The testimonies to other writers getting some of their best ideas away from their desks are plentiful, but then you have R. L. Stein who, when asked, "Do you ever incorporate any of your own experiences into your books?" says this in response: "Believe it or not, I've never written about any of my experiences. I don't have too many experiences because I never leave the house! I'm here

Thinking It Through...

You might look at the list of understandings and strategies above and see what connections you make. Have you had any writing experiences that led you to similar understandings or to use similar strategies? Do you see any disconnections— things that don't ring as true for you from your own writing experience?

writing every day" (Scholastic website). Now, while I'm sure R. L. Stein may be overstating the case a little bit, the fact is this author says he gets most of his ideas right there at home while working at his desk on his writing. I need to know this. I need to know that from time to time I might meet other writers in my teaching who get many of their ideas more like R. L. Stein does than like Katie Ray does.

The poet Patricia Hubbell gets many of her best ideas away from the desk, and she also uses a strategy just like mine to save them: *if you think of something good, keep repeating it so you won't lose it before you can get to some paper to write it down.* This is what she says about it:

> I also get ideas while I'm out for a walk or riding my horse. Unfortunately, if I'm on my horse, the idea has to wait until I get home before I can write it down. While I ride I keep saying the idea over and over in my head to be sure I don't lose it. There's nothing more frustrating than losing a line or an idea and never getting it back. (Copeland and Copeland 1994, 154)

Horseback riding or motorcycle riding, the strategy is a good one if you can't exactly stop and write at that moment.

Because I am such a fan of her writing, I was thrilled to learn that Naomi Shihab Nye talks to herself when writing just like I do. I like to share this connection with students when teaching them to *try composing lines out loud (in different ways) to see how they sound.* I tell them my story of doing this, but then I also tell them what Naomi says, "I think I was always talking to myself back then, as I do now, without apology, shaping words, hearing conversant language inside my head" (Nye 1999).

Again, what's important about finding connections and *dis*connections in the study of process is seeing how the work of writers is manifested in different ways in different writing lives. With our study of process we are helping students find ways *to be* as writers, and the more possibilities we open for them to see, the more fullness there will be to their becoming writers.

ENVISION your students doing "this" or thinking "this" as they write

The guiding questions here are, "What would it look like if my students tried this (a strategy)?" or "What might happen if my students understood this (an understanding)?" We have to be able to envision what difference this curriculum might make in our students' writing lives. This is critical to our teaching. We always finish conferences or minilessons by helping students envision using a certain understanding or strategy in their own writing work. We just paint a little picture with words to help them see what a strategy or understanding could look like if it happened in a totally different context than the one where it happened to us. We just make things up like this, untying what happened to us from its context and imagining it happening to someone else in a whole different context.

Let's take just a few of the curriculum chunks we've named in this one story and I'll show how I might envision them for students at the very end of a minilesson or conference. I'll write them as I would actually say them when teaching. Notice that I actually make up a real, living scenario that could happen to another writer. Sometimes I even make up some text to go with the example, if it makes sense for what we are envisioning. Each one of these would be a *different* instance of teaching, depending on which aspect of process I am wanting to highlight. I have put some of the ones that are closely related together as I would likely be combining them in the same minilesson or conference.

Sometimes writers get their best ideas far away from the desk.

"Ya'll really need to think about this. You go so many places where there are writing ideas all around you—just like there were for me on that motorcycle that day.

Just think, you could be at baseball practice and you see a storm coming in the distance. You realize that storms always seem to come from exactly that same place, they always seem to gather just over the outfield bleachers. But because you are a writer, you also think, *Hmm…this could be the beginning of something. Storms always coming from the same place.* Those kinds of noticings need to go in your notebook."

Sometimes ideas come to you in the form of perfect titles.

"Let's say you are out camping one evening and you look up and notice stars and you think they look like holes punched in the sky. And then you think to yourself, *Hmm … Holes Punched in a Night Sky. What a great title that would be for something. I better write this down.* Be sure you don't lose those titles."

Sometimes you can see different potentials for revision and punctuation by reading lines out loud in different ways.
Try composing lines out loud (in different ways) to see how they sound.

"I can see some of you doing exactly what I did—playing around with lines that come to you when you are far away from our workshop. Like maybe you're in the bathtub thinking of lines for a story about NASCAR and you just try saying them different ways out loud. *Like thunder from the distance, getting closer, the cars speed by me. Like distant thunder, getting closer, the cars speed by me. The cars speed by, distant thunder. Coming closer.* Like that. You just try it out and see how it sounds different ways when you move the language and the punctuation around."

If you think of something good, keep repeating it so you won't lose it before you can get to some paper to write it down.

"As diligent as we all are about having our notebooks with us at all times, this is going to happen to every one of us at some time or another. Some great words are going to come to us and we will be in a situation where we simply can't write at that moment—not even on a scrap of paper or a napkin. You might be in the middle of a marching band performance when the perfect ending to your editorial just comes to you. You could be out on a hike, notebook forgotten and no writing implements in sight when, bam, a line for a poem just comes and won't leave. Try doing what I did. Just keep saying it over and over, as much as you need to, until you know you've memorized it and won't lose it before you get to paper. If you're not alone and can talk to someone else, tell that person too and let him or her help you remember. Just don't lose those words!"

Try making a list if you are trying to get a lot of separate ideas down fast—you can figure out how they go together later.

"This little strategy is so helpful because sometimes ideas just come to us faster than we can organize them. For me this happened because I had actually been thinking about this for some time before I got to my notebook. For you, it could be that reason, or it might be that they're coming fast for some other reason. Maybe someone is talking, like in an interview on ESPN or something, and you think it's interesting and are trying to get it all down fast. Just list it. Or maybe you wake up in the middle of a dream and are trying—desperately before you lose it—to remember all the details of the dream. Just list them very fast."

As we see from these examples, we really want to think all the way *into* the writing lives of our students as we offer them this curriculum of process. We want to make it so they can picture it, so they can see themselves thinking like this or doing this—whatever the "this" may be—as writers themselves. We use what we know about their lives both inside school and outside school to help us craft these visions for them as we teach.

So there we have it. A line of thinking that begins with telling the stories of our writing experiences and ends with the development of writing curriculum that we can actually envision our students using in their work. When in use, this line of thinking is actually much more recursive than it is linear, much like the writing process itself. We move around the line—noticing, connecting, describing, envisioning, naming—as we think about our own writing experiences. But the parts of the line are all there in our thinking as we write like teachers of writing.

References

Copeland, Jeffrey S., and Vicky L. Copeland. 1994. "Patrician Hubbell." In *Speaking of Poets 2: More Interviews with Poets Who Write for Children and Young Adults.* Urbana, IL: NCTE.

Letts, Billie. 1995. *Where the Heart Is.* New York: Warner.

Locker, Thomas. 1997. *Water Dance.* New York: Harcourt Brace.

Nye, Naomi Shihab. Spring 1999. "My First True Love." In *CBC Features* (52) 1. New York: The Children's Book Council, Inc.

Powell, Dannye Romine. 1995. "Lee Smith." In *Parting the Curtains: Voices of the Great Southern Writers.* New York: Anchor Books.

Ray, Katie Wood. 1999. *Wondrous Words: Writers and Writing in the Elementary Classroom.* Urbana, IL: NCTE.

Rylant, Cynthia. 1996. *The Whales.* New York: Blue Sky Press.

Stein, R. L. "Authors and Books–Author Studies–R. L. Stein–Interview Transcript." Retrieved from www.scholastic.com

CHAPTER 3

Getting Started Developing the Curriculum of Process

We are teachers of writing, but many of us are also teachers of science and math and social studies, most of us are husbands, wives, partners, mothers, daughters, friends, golfers, joggers, gardeners . . . we're busy, in other words. We don't have all the time in the world to be writers, so we have to be purposeful and selective about the writing we do to support our teaching. Because at least one purpose in writing ourselves is to understand what it is we are teaching students how to do, we select our own writing engagements based on this. Over time we make sure we have tried the things we will ask students to try in our writing workshops.

To get started with curriculum development for writing process, then, we need to first name the process we'll be teaching students to use for writing. Many of us have developed our knowledge base for this process from our studies of professional writers and what they say about bringing pieces of writing into being. From these studies we know that we have to teach students how to do basically three main things:

- ◆ Get ideas for writing and keep up with those ideas
- ◆ Select ideas to "grow" into published pieces of writing
- ◆ Draft, revise, and edit for publication

As teachers of writing, we'll need some experience with each part of this process if we are to understand what we are trying to teach students how to do. As we engage in this process, our two main questions of process will guide us:

What kinds of things do writers think about and why do they think about these things?

What kinds of things do writers do and how and why do they do them?

Let's think this process through a little and imagine the kinds of things we might do to help us with curriculum development.

Getting Ideas for Writing and Keeping Up with Those Ideas

One of the very first things we have to teach our students is how to find ideas for writing. When most of us were in school, the question of where we would get our ideas for writing was never really an issue. Because we were usually given topics for writing, the part of the process where you first get ideas was completely skipped over in the teaching of writing most of us knew as students.

In writing workshops today, though, things look a lot different. We believe that it is only by working through the whole process of writing from ideas to publication that students will get the much needed experience to become proficient writers. We realize that in the whole of this process, the beginning point is in the getting of ideas, something we insist students learn to do for themselves. And because we expect students to have active publishing lives, we have to support them with lots of solid curriculum that helps them answer perhaps the most fundamental of all questions about the writing process: "Where will I get my ideas for writing?"

One of the biggest misconceptions about this part of the writing process is that writers get ideas sitting at desks. That "they think them up out of their heads," as one little boy once told me. From professionals we've learned that writers get ideas everywhere, and mostly away from their desks—waiting in checkout lines at the grocery store, driving in their cars, listening to the radio, walking the dog. Writers don't need to live more extraordinary lives than other people, they simply need to see their lives differently because of who they are: writers, who need ideas. Ralph Fletcher explains it this way in his wonderful little book *A Writer's Notebook: Unlocking the Writer Within You*: "Writers are like other people, except for at least one important difference. Other people have daily thoughts and feelings, notice this sky or that smell, but they don't do much about it. All those thoughts, feelings, sensations, and opinions pass through them like the air they breath. Not writers. Writers react"(Fletcher 1996b, 3).

For most writers, that reaction is to write it down, whatever the "it" may be—an interesting tidbit we've overheard, a question that's just occurred to us, a fascinating play of light on oil on water in our driveway. Anything. We just write it down. We never know what might come of it, and we have to get some ideas, some material we can work with in our writing.

As teachers of writing, then, we try living in the world and reacting as writers do. We react and we see what it *feels* like to place our faith in the idea that these reactions can become writing possibilities. We see what we *think about* as we move through the world, reacting and gathering those reactions. We see what kinds of things it occurs to us *to do* as we live this way. And for a while, at first, we just have to do it. We have to live in the world as writers say they live—noticing, questioning, eavesdropping, observing, dreaming. We try and remember what Anne Lamott says as we live this writing life, "I think this is how we are supposed to be in the world—present and in awe" (1994, 100). We try this life on for size, the one we are wanting to teach our students how to live.

A writer's notebook is a convenient tool many professional writers use to keep up with all the ideas they find in the world, and many of us teachers of writing have our students use notebooks as well. The first curriculum development many of us do, then, is to start our own writers' notebooks where we try and gather ideas from the world around us. We try gathering different kinds entries in the ways we'll expect students to gather them. We try getting ideas from

- ◆ Things we see that are interesting
- ◆ Very close observations of things, capturing sights, sounds, textures, moods, etc.
- ◆ Snippets of interesting dialogue we have eavesdropped on
- ◆ Questions about a subject, a person, a thing, a place, etc.
- ◆ Lists of things we might want to think about later
- ◆ Quotations from music, film, literature, pop culture, etc. that interest us
- ◆ Writing generated from photographs that interest us
- ◆ Things we remember about our lives in the past
- ◆ Plot ideas from news blurbs we hear or real-life scenarios we know about
- ◆ Character ideas from interesting people we see
- ◆ Setting ideas from places where we are writing
- ◆ Entries about things that interest us as people
- ◆ Research data about things of interest to us
- ◆ Reflections on and off things we see, hear, or think about. When you reflect *on* it, you stay with it; when you reflect *off* it, you let your mind go wherever it leads you. In one, you purposefully focus. In the other, you purposefully wander.
- ◆ Word-play with words we like
- ◆ Family stories that we know
- ◆ Writing generated from conversations we've had
- ◆ Lists of people or place names that we like that we might use some day
- ◆ Entries about things we care about

This is a good beginning list of the many kinds of things we find in a writer's notebook, the kinds of things we might try ourselves as writers and then teach to our students. And while there are common kinds of entries writers collect in notebooks, we'll want to remember that ideas come to us in a rich variety of ways when we are on the lookout for them. As teachers of writing, we start our own writer's notebooks knowing that, along with our students, we will invent ways of using them that we would never have thought about when we first started.

Sometimes we'll want to make very purposeful entries in our notebooks, and we'll ask students to do the same. If we know we are going to be doing a particular kind of writing, for instance, then we'll need to keep our notebooks for a while as writers of that genre. We'll focus on the kinds of entries that are likely to generate good material for that genre—lots of things we remember for memoir; lots of observations and reflections for poetry; responses to news items and conversations for editorials; plot, character and setting ideas for fiction, etc.

Our writers' notebooks will become one of the most important curriculum documents we have for the teaching of writing. Just a few predictable questions about our own writing experiences with notebooks can help us find all the curriculum we need for this part of the process: getting ideas and keeping up with them. Certain important curricular "themes" will show up again and again as we embed the answers to the following questions in our minilessons (as we'll see in the next chapter). As we look back over the entries in our writing notebooks, we look at them as *stories about our writing lives* and we ask these kinds of questions about those stories:

> ### Thinking It Through... ↺
>
> *If you already have a writer's notebook or some collection of ideas for writing, look at what you have and try framing some stories about collecting those ideas by answering the questions at the top of page 36. What curriculum understandings or strategies come out of your stories? If you haven't been collecting ideas for writing, remember you don't need a new life! You just need to pay attention to the one you've got. To get started, try it for just 24 hours. Pay attention and write some ideas down. Then use the questions at the top of page 36 to tell your beginning stories of living in the world as a writer and start digging out the curriculum of this part of the process.*

Telling the stories of our notebook entries...	...leads us to curricular themes.
Where was I when had the idea for writing this entry?	Writers get ideas in all kinds of places.
What was I doing when I stopped to write this entry?	Sometimes we get ideas for writing when we're not writing. Sometimes we just write. Notebooks travel.
What prompted me to write this entry?	Seeing potential in an idea. Blind faith in the process of gathering. Purposeful gathering. Purposeful trying.
How is this entry written? Why did I write it this way?	Different formats entries can take. How form follows function in entries. Purposeful trying.
What happened in my thinking as I was writing this?	Writing things down leads to more thinking. Writing and thinking about writing happen simultaneously.
What can I imagine doing with this entry?	Material gathered in notebooks is used to support a published writing life as opposed to a writing life you keep to yourself in a journal or diary. Published means you get pieces ready for audiences—ready to go public.

Selecting Ideas to Grow into Published Pieces of Writing

Every published piece of writing we see began at some time with a writer deciding to pursue a particular idea through drafting, revising, and editing until that idea was a finished piece of writing. Many teachers call these beginning ideas "seed ideas," and the pursuit of a finished piece they call having "a writing project." A writer's notebook can fill up quickly with all kinds of writing possibilities, but at some point writers have to make decisions about which ideas they'll pursue as writing projects. Again, most of us never had experience with this decision-making part of the writing process when we were in school, so we experience it for the first time as teachers of writing.

Seed ideas for writing projects have lots of different origins. Sometimes they start with a notebook idea that just won't leave a writer alone—a particular way the clouds looked on a rainy afternoon, an old man sitting by the side of the road selling honey, a conversation about life that keeps the writer thinking. It's an idea that makes us think: *there just has to be something I could do with this.*

Sometimes seed ideas just naturally grow out of passions and interests in our lives—our children, basketball, rain forests, cooking, stars, and planets. We have notebooks full of entries about these things we love in life, and it just makes sense that some writing projects will grow from what we know best. Sometimes seed ideas actually come to us as audiences and occasions we *need* to write for rather than as topics for writing—anniversaries, birthdays, bar mitzvahs, and graduations for relatives, friends, and family. We begin these writing projects with the audience and occasion in mind. Sometimes we have causes we need to address and so we start letters and editorials and campaigns as writing projects.

> ### Thinking It Through...
>
> Think back to writing you have done on your own outside of school. Where did your seed ideas come from for this writing? Why did you decide to pursue these pieces of writing? What do your answers to these questions tell you about why writers choose to pursue writing projects?

Sometimes seed ideas for writing projects are found because writers are wanting (or are required) to do a certain kind of writing. "I've never written fiction," the writer thinks, and so she begins keeping her notebook and searching her previous entries like a writer of fiction. When we organize genre studies in our classrooms and expect our students to publish pieces in this genre, we necessarily require them to find seed ideas that lend themselves to writing in this genre.

Thinking It Through... ⟲

Go ahead and use the entries in your notebook to think about this question: "What's in here that I might pursue as a writing project?" Also, just think about your life in general. Do you have any ideas (that aren't in your notebook) for writing projects that you might like to pursue? Why would you want to pursue these projects? What does that tell you about how writers choose projects? You can think about this even if you haven't started your 24 hours notebook yet.

As teachers of writing, then, we search our writers' notebooks with this question in mind, "What's in here that I might pursue as a writing project?" We think about this question as if we were full-time writers who had to sustain active publishing lives, because this is how we will ask our students to think of themselves.

Now, here's a little secret about curriculum development in this area. We can actually teach lots of minilessons and conferences on how to find seed ideas by simply taking the time to answer this question from our notebooks. We don't actually even have to draft all the seed ideas we find. We only have to be able to imagine drafting and publishing them to teach from them. It's *how* a writer might choose that we are teaching. Some of them we'll need to pursue so we can explore the remaining parts of the process, but lots of them we can simply think through as seed idea possibilities. The sample minilesson in the next chapter about writing a piece about tiny, wondrous things in nature is a perfect example of a piece of writing I've dreamed of drafting and publishing but never actually started. I dreamed it, and now I teach about choosing seed ideas from that dream.

Once we have a notebook with a good collection of ideas in it, we'll want to spend time finding seed ideas in our material and thinking of the writing projects we could do from them. Sometimes we'll know a lot about the kind of writing we want to do when we choose a seed idea (I want to write a collection of poems about my niece for her eleventh birthday), and sometimes we'll know very little (I want to write something about my experiences in Africa, but I have no idea what). We'll want to remember there are often numerous writing projects we might dream of doing from a single seed idea. If basketball is our passion, for instance, we might imagine doing several collections of basketball poetry, a memoir about learning to play basketball, a feature article on our favorite NBA player, a fictional short story about a basketball team, and on and on. If writers can envision lots of different kinds of writing projects, they really only need a few good seed ideas. We don't have to have a new "topic" every time we set out to write.

As we find seed ideas for writing projects from our own notebooks, we'll want to ask a few predictable questions about these ideas that will help us frame our minilessons and embed the important curricular themes for this part of the writing process:

Telling the story of finding seed ideas...	...leads us to curricular themes.
How and why did I first decide to work on this project?	Writers decide to work on projects for a variety of reasons.
What did I know about the idea when I first made the decision?	Sometimes writers know a lot about a project at the start, sometimes they know very little.
What role, if any, did my notebook play in the decision to work on this project?	Sometimes writers find project ideas in notebooks. Sometimes writers bring project ideas to notebooks.

Once we have seed ideas, our next job is to think about how we can use our notebooks to "grow" them before we actually begin our drafts. Inexperienced writers often want to move straight from seed ideas to drafts. And sometimes drafts do just "come" to writers and the seed idea itself is really a beginning draft. But we also know that many professional writers actually grow their ideas for a long, long time before they ever move to draft them. Many teachers call this part of the writing process "nurturing," and they know that students need lots of solid curriculum to teach them how to nurture an idea before drafting it. We need to try this part of the process because, yet again, many of us have had very little experience with it ourselves.

Thinking It Through...

Take some of the seed ideas you thought about earlier and use the list below (and your own strategies) to imagine some ways you might nurture them before drafting them. Why do you think this nurturing work you've imagined makes sense for your seed ideas? What do you think might come of it? What does this tell you about how a writer chooses how to nurture and grow a seed idea?

Nurturing often happens in the writer's notebook. In *Breathing In, Breathing Out*, Ralph Fletcher says the notebook "gives you a place to incubate very new ideas before they are strong and mature enough to face the harsh light of rational judgment, let alone public scrutiny" (1996a, 1–2). Our young writers need to know how to "incubate" their ideas, what it might look like when a writer is doing this nurturing. It can take many forms, but here are just a few of the kinds of things writers can do to grow seed ideas before drafting them:

- ◆ Extend entries related to the seed idea by writing "off" words in the entries—purposefully wander in your writing
- ◆ Ask questions about the idea and try and answer those questions in writing
- ◆ Keep lists of all ideas related to the seed idea
- ◆ Talk to others about the seed idea and write "off" that talk
- ◆ Collect artifacts related to the seed idea and write "off" those
- ◆ Read books on a topic, a person, a time period, etc. and make notes of ideas, facts
- ◆ Observe in settings related to the seed idea and write from these observations
- ◆ Conduct firsthand research around the seed idea—surveys, interviews, etc.
- ◆ Experiment with writing about the seed idea in different genres
- ◆ Get to know characters (for fiction)
- ◆ Map out different possibilities for organizing different kinds of drafts of the idea

- ◆ Try various beginnings, endings, lines
- ◆ Imagine the idea written in different structures
- ◆ Imagine the idea written in different voices

As teachers of writing, we will need to do some of this work with seed ideas that we are going to take through the whole of the writing process. We can, however, simply imagine what work we *would* do for the seed ideas we have found but probably won't pursue for publication. Again, in the sample mini-lesson on tiny, wondrous things in nature in the next chapter, you can see that I imagined what work I would need to do to develop the idea before drafting it. For the seed ideas we do choose to grow in our notebooks, here are some predictable questions that will help us frame our minilessons and embed the important curricular themes for this part of the writing process:

Telling the story of growing seed ideas...	...leads us to curricular themes.
What kind of writing work did I do before I began drafting this project?	Writers prewrite around an idea (in a variety of ways) before drafting it.
How did I decide to do this writing work?	Writers know what kinds of material they will need to begin drafting. Writers trust ideas to grow.
What kinds of nonwriting work did I do for this project?	Writers do all kinds of writing-related work (research, interview, observe, collect, etc.) to support a project.
How did I imagine using all this work to help me with the project?	Writers have a sense of why they are doing the work they are doing.

Drafting, Revising, and Editing for Publication

The move from writing in a notebook about a seed idea to beginning a draft is a tricky move for many writers, and it's one we'll need to experience as teachers of writing to really understand. Most of us did write drafts when we were in school, but the process wasn't much like the one we ask students to go through today. More often than not, we were told how we should draft the topics we'd been given, how long they should be, and what parts they should include in the fill-in-the-blank outlines we were given for our drafts. We want to teach ourselves and our students to begin drafts the way writers in the world outside school begin them, and this means we and our students will have to make lots of decisions on our own that our teachers made for us. This will make our drafting more challenging in many ways.

What's the difference between writing about a seed idea in a notebook and beginning a draft? Beginning a draft means that as writers we have begun to *make something*. It's something real, something we can picture. It's like something we have read: "I'm writing a short piece of personal narrative like they have in the back of *Southern Living*. I'm making a series of books like the Junie B. Jones series by Barbara Park. I am writing my memoirs as a series of poems like Lee Bennett Hopkins did in *Been to Yesterdays* (1995) and Lessie Jones Little did in *Children of Long Ago* (2000). I'm going to put together a collage of writing like Charles Smith did in *Rimshots* (1999) . . . " There is such a different energy when we feel like we're making something, and this is the energy that fuels the move from notebooks to drafts.

I know about this energy because I've felt it in my own writing experience, and it guides my teaching of drafting in so many ways. Recently while conferring with some high school students, I sat down next to a young woman who was writing a piece about Mr. Rogers. She told me a little of the story of her idea. She heard on the news that he was retiring, and she thought about how sad that was because she kind of grew up with *Mr. Rogers' Neighborhood*, so she decided to do a piece of writing about him.

She pulled out all these research notes she had on him and a draft she had started that was about a page and a half at this point. When I asked her what *kind* of writing it was, she didn't really have an answer. I led her a little bit and gave her some choices. "Is it more like a story, or an essay, or article? What have you read that this is like?" I asked her. And I could tell from that look she got in her eyes that she made an answer up (you know how they do that when you're conferring?).

She said, "I don't know, I guess it's kind of like an article?"

So I asked her, "Well, would it be the kind of thing you would read in a newspaper or a magazine or what exactly?"

She made another answer up. "A magazine," she said.

I pushed some more. "Okay. Well would it be more like *Time* magazine and *Newsweek*, or more like *Ladies Home Journal* or *Redbook*? What *kind* of magazine?" I asked her.

She made another answer up, but this time with gusto. "*Glamour* magazine," she said. I smiled as I imagined Mr. Rogers appearing in the fashion do's and don'ts or in a feature article about how to land a "boy next door" or some other, more risqué *Glamour*-type article.

This line of questioning gave this young writer an image of what she was making, an image that she made up as we went along, but it was this image that gave her energy. I don't think she had ever really thought about what she was writing in this way. She'd never really thought about, "What kind of thing am I making and where would it fit in the world?" Once she did, like all writers, she began to draft very differently. She drafted with a clear sense of what she was trying to make.

When we start a draft, then, we have started to make something; and as we revise this draft along the way, we'll revise with this image of what we're making very clearly in our minds. Sometimes we know a lot about how we want the finished piece to be when we start drafting, and sometimes we figure it out along the way, but at some point in the process, we have to know what kind of writing "thing" it is that we're making with our project. We'll need to know two main things about it: what genre it will be and what approach to the writing we'll use. These are separate questions because a decision about genre doesn't imply a single kind of writing. We may decide, for example, that the piece of writing is going to be memoir, but then we have to decide how we'll write this memoir—as a series of poems, as short and separate vignettes, as a long and continuous story, or in some other fashion. Is it the kind of thing that would be published as a picture book, in a magazine, as a chapter book, a coffee table book, or what? Who's the audience? Children, adults, family, strangers?

Thinking It Through...

Okay, now take some of your seed ideas and think specifically about what kinds of writing you might make with these ideas. Try and name specific published writing you have read that is like what you would be trying. Who would your audience be? Think about why you would want to write your ideas in these ways. What does your thinking tell you about how writers decide what kind of writing to do—once they have a seed idea?

As teachers of writing, we will need to take a few of the seed ideas we have grown in our notebooks and make this move to draft them into pieces of published writing. At some point, we'll need to try this arbitrarily and let the seed idea itself determine the kind of writing it becomes. We'll also want to do what we'll ask our students to do from time to time and set out to draft pieces in specific genres, knowing this from the very start before we even select and grow the seed ideas. We'll want to make sure that we have drafted at least one piece of writing in any genre we are going to teach our students so that we'll have at least one experience in which we can anchor our teaching. It may take awhile to get pieces written in a variety of genres, but once we do, we can teach from the experience of this for a long time.

As we draft, we have to remember to keep up with decisions we are making along the way. Word processors are fabulous tools for drafting and revision because they allow us to change and manipulate text so easily, but as teaching tools they can be disastrous because they erase all evidence of our revision. We have to be careful to notice when we are making a drafting or revision decision that would be good curriculum. We'll want to make note of it somehow and keep a record of the before-and-after of it. If we are drafting on word processors, we'll want to print them out often and make notes about the "story" of the drafting in the margins.

Sometimes we might actually draft and revise with a particular thing in mind, paying attention to how we do something so we can better explain it to students. I recently had to do this with paragraph breaks. I was conferring with some older writers who were writing very long texts and not breaking them into paragraphs in their drafts. When I asked them why, they explained that they were going to go back and put the paragraph breaks in later. This was curious to me because I write long texts and I know that I make paragraph breaks as I go. But when I launched into an explanation of how I know where to put them, I realized I didn't have anything very articulate I could say about it. I needed to study this as a teacher of writing and figure out how I know where paragraph breaks go.

With drafting and revision, then, we'll want to pay attention to the in-process kinds of things that happen as we write, but we'll also want to experiment with different tools for revision that we learn from professional writers or invent for ourselves. Here are just a few revision tools (gathered from many sources through the years) we might try with our drafts and then teach to our students as possibilities:

◆ Take a line and use my notebook to try writing it lots of different ways.
◆ Find all the verbs in the draft and ask, "Is there a more precise verb I might use?"
◆ Have someone read the draft and then give a summary of it. Ask myself, "Did my piece make sense to this reader?"
◆ Consider shifting the voice of the piece by changing the person of the pronouns.
◆ Reread and box the draft into "chunks." Do the chunks work? Might they be rearranged? Do I move from one to the next smoothly? Are

there any other structures I could put in place to make the piece work more effectively?

- Take a small chunk and write it longer (add inside thinking, add an image, slow time down). Take a long chunk and make it shorter (say a lot in one sentence, speed time up).
- Try starting the draft in a different place.
- Try crafting techniques in the draft that I've seen other authors use in other texts.
- Look closely at punctuation. Are there places where I could exploit punctuation marks to help make my meaning stronger?
- Consider paragraph breaks. Are they effective? There are many ways to divide a piece into paragraphs. Use these divisions to make meaning.
- Cut out absolutely, positively anything I can from the draft. Prune it back.
- Add anything that would make the meaning stronger.
- Read the draft aloud, over and over. *Listen* for what I need to do to it.

Drafting and revision are all about making the writing match the vision we have for it as closely as possible. Editing, which we do all along the way, is really more a matter of proofreading the piece, grooming it for our readers. Readers expect us to have been over our drafts with a fine-toothed comb and gotten everything in order. Readers respond to our writing more positively when they can tell we've done this. We'll want to pay close attention to *how* we edit, what kinds of things we think about and what kinds of things we do to get this job accomplished. We'll also need to remember that writers can't edit for things they don't know, so we'll have to look closely at students' writing to see what curriculum of conventions they need along with the curriculum of process for editing.

Thinking It Through...

To really study the drafting and editing process, you have to jump in and start a draft. Old drafts don't work as well for this study because we don't remember what we were thinking as we drafted. So jump in, play around with a beginning draft, and then use the following questions to study your process. Remember to capture your thinking as you go.

As we move from notebooks to drafting, revising, and editing, here are some of the predictable questions we'll ask that will help us frame our mini-lessons and embed the important curricular themes for this part of the writing process:

Telling the story of drafting...	...leads us to curricular themes.
At what point did I start the draft? Why did I decide to start?	Writers begin drafting for a variety of reasons.
What did I know about the draft before I started it?	Sometimes writers know a lot about how a draft will go, sometimes they know very little about how it will go.
How, EXACTLY, did I get started?	Writers draft in different ways.
How did I use my notebook to help me draft?	Writers incorporate material and ideas they have gathered into drafts in different ways.
What kind of things happened as I was drafting?	The process of drafting is rarely smooth.
What, other than writing, did I do as I was drafting?	Writers interrupt drafting for a variety of reasons: to read their drafts, to take a break, to get someone else to read it, etc.
What revisions did I make as I was drafting? What, exactly, caused me to make these revisions?	Many writers actually revise as they are drafting.
What, exactly, did I do with the draft after it was completed? Why?	Writers have a variety of tools and strategies for revising and editing drafts.
How did I know this draft was ready to be published?	Writers stop work and declare pieces "finished" for a variety of reasons.

Living the Life of a Writer

In our classrooms, as we ask students to write every single day and publish a lot during the year, we also will be asking them to create a writing life for themselves. A person can't do something every single day without that happening, without coming to know himself or herself in that way. So as we do some

Telling the story of our writing lives...	...leads us to curricular themes.
What kinds of things do I write? Why?	A writer's "world" work is strongly influenced by the kind of writing he or she does, and vice versa.
How do I use other people to support my writing life?	Many writers are members of response groups, get feedback from trusted friends and family, etc.
What kinds of writing do I see myself working on in the future?	Writers live with a sense of the future and what they will be working on next.
How is reading a part of my writing life?	Writers are also readers.
What else in my "other" life feeds my writing life?	A life outside writing is necessary to sustain the writing.
How does what I have published in the past influence my present?	Publishing is a commitment. Writers are responsible for their words in the world.
What is it that keeps me writing?	Writers continue to publish for a variety of reasons.
What are my strengths as a writer? Weaknesses?	Writers exploit their strengths and manage their weaknesses.
What kinds of things do I do to make myself a better writer?	Writers work at their craft.
What are my habits as a writer?	Writers find ways of working that help them get their writing done.

writing ourselves, over time we'll want to think about our own writing lives and the curriculum that is embedded in what we understand about ourselves as writers. We'll remember, of course, that our lives represent only one way to be as writers and that we'll need our students and our co-teachers of writing to show us other ways to be, but our knowing about the writing life begins with our own experiences. We can ask ourselves these kinds of questions from time to time as we think about the curriculum of living a writing life (see page 48).

Again, we're all very busy and we have to go at this writing thing with both a spirit of adventure and a clear sense of realism. It may take several years to get a good collection of our own writing experiences we can use in our teaching. But we stay at it, and we teach with the music in front of us until we get to that place where we can teach *by heart*.

References

Fletcher, Ralph. 1996a. *Breathing In, Breathing Out: Keeping a Writer's Notebook*. Portsmouth, NH: Heinemann.

———. 1996b. *A Writer's Notebook: Unlocking the Writer Within You*. New York: Avon Books.

Hopkins, Lee Bennet. 1995. *Been to Yesterdays: Poems of a Life*. Illustrations by Charlene Rendeiro. Honesdale, PA: Wordsong, Boyds Mills Press.

Lamott, Anne. 1994. *Bird by Bird: Some Instructions on Writing and Life*. New York: Pantheon Books.

Little, Lessie Jones. 2000. *Children of Long Ago*. Illustrated by Jan Spivey Gilchrist. New York: Lee & Low Books.

Park, Barbara. *Junie B. Jones* series. Illustrated by Denise Brunkus. New York: Random House.

Smith, Charles R. 1999. *Rimshots: Basketball Pix, Rolls, and Rhythms*. New York: Dutton Children's Books.

CHAPTER 4

Looking Closely at Minilessons
Teaching from Our Own Writing

In many ways, we have to become good storytellers if we want to teach minilessons of process from our own writing. As we explained in Chapter Three, layers of strategies and understandings about the process of writing are embedded in any single story from our writing lives. When we teach minilessons, we choose a curricular focus for the lesson, a specific thing we are teaching that fits into a series of minilessons, and then we tell the writing story around it. As we embed the answers to many of our essential questions (detailed in the last chapter), we trust the story to do all kinds of teaching beyond the specific focus of the lesson. We trust the "underneath curriculum" layered into the story and know that, over time, as students hear lots of writing stories in minilessons and conferences, they will be exposed again and again to some of the most essential curriculum of process.

Sample Minilesson on a Notebook Strategy

To illustrate this, let's look closely at some sample minilessons about different parts of the writing process. The focus of this first minilesson is a strategy: *try rewriting an existing entry and crafting it to sound like literature*. This is what would be written in the lesson plans as the objective. The lesson would be one of a series of lessons that show students ways to experiment in their writers' notebooks and try new writing "off" the writing they have there. Notice, however, all the rich curriculum embedded in the story about how a writing life is lived, where writers get ideas, and how one keeps a writer's notebook. We'll put the text of the actual minilesson on the right, and on the left we'll name the "chunks" of curriculum embedded in the story.

Curriculum Chunks	Minilesson Text
	I know that at this point most of you have a lot of entries you've gathered in your notebooks over the last few weeks. Most all of you have really neat stuff that you've gathered and written both in class and outside of class. This made me think that it was probably time to start showing you some things you can do to build more writing out of the writing you already have. That's the neat thing about keeping a notebook: once you get a few entries in there, you can just go on and on building new entries out of those because you've always got stuff to work with.
Sometimes writers make new writing out of existing writing.	
Writers have strategies they like to use.	The strategy I want to show you today is actually one I really like to try myself as a writer. I used it not long ago. First, I was in my office and had some time so I was looking for some writing work I could do. I started by rereading my notebook and just looking at different entries I had there. I came across this one I had written after my husband and I spent the day at the lake. I saw some very fascinating water bugs while I was sitting on my jet ski waiting for him to bring the trailer around. I watched them and they were just so marvelous; so as soon as I got in the truck and got dried off, I got my notebook and I wrote an entry that simply described them as best I could. I was trying to get down as much detail as I could in this first entry, and it was written very fast with very
Sometimes writers make work for themselves.	
Sometimes writers reread their notebooks for ideas.	
Writers get ideas in all kinds of places.	
One type of entry writers collect is an observation of something that fascinates them.	

Curriculum Chunks

*Notebooks travel away from our desks.

*If you want to get it down with detail before you forget it, try writing it very fast first, with no attention to sound.

*Sometimes great lines just come to you when writing.

*Sometimes writers play around in their notebooks.

*Writers know the sound of language in books they admire.

*Try reading some literature that sounds like what you want to write, before you start writing.

*Try extending a metaphor as one option for making writing sound more like literature.

*Literature (crafted writing) sounds different than just fast writing in a notebook.

*Sometimes writers come back to things that have potential.

*Writers have dreams of things they'd like to publish someday.

Minilesson Text

little attention to how the words sounded. I just wanted to write it fast before I forgot what it looked like. Let me show you. [Show or read students the notebook entry shown in Figure 4–1 on page 53.]

So I came across this entry as I was rereading and I liked the line in it, "water bugs skate on a mirror of lake"— which is a line that just came to me as I was watching them that day at the lake. I decided that for my writing work that day I was going to try writing it again, but this time I wanted it to sound more like literature. I thought it would be fun to play around and try giving it the sound of some of those kinds of books I really like, those really descriptive ones like *Canoe Days* by Gary Paulsen (1999) and *Scarecrow* by Cynthia Rylant (1998). So first I got those two books and I read some of them to myself out loud—just to get the sound in my head. Then, I started rewriting the entry. I flipped back and forth between the first pages where I'd written it and the new entry where I was really trying to get the words to sound more like literature. I tried to extend that metaphor a little from the line that had just come to me—water bugs as skaters. The whole time I was writing the second, more literature-like entry, I was keeping in my head the sound of those books I was trying to write like. Here's what I came up with. [Show or read entry shown in Figure 4–2 on page 54.]

I really liked trying this and I can even see some potential in this. It's something I might come back to sometime and work on more. I've always wanted to publish something like this as a picture book—something kind of quiet and beautiful about nature. But the thing is, this is a strategy some of you might want to try: finding an entry you like and then rewriting it with the sound of some literature in your head. If you decide to try it, you'll first need to reread your notebook and look for an entry that

Waterbugs Skate
in a manner of like...

At Keowee, while I sat in my jet ski and waited for Jim to bring the truck around, I watched this whole — I don't know — clan? of these amazing waterbugs. They are almost ALL legs. They have these tiny little bodies and then these LONG slender legs that stick out awkwardly off the sides. They look sort of like those oil rig boat in the ocean. And they have these really weird movements. They seem to make these really quick glides. And they can go (I think they are 90° angles (I think they are 90° degrees — I need to look that up) But they more really fast at these very odd angles and their legs don't seem to move really at all. I would love to know exactly how they do it.

And I think it's because the movement probably happens so fast you just can't see it. And the other flurry thing is that there were a whole lot of these water bugs (is that really their name?) all in this one central spot in the water, all moving really fast. And it would look like they were going to crash right into each other right at the last moment, just before the almost certain collision, they would dart in opposite direction and avoid disaster. It's like they are playing that old game of chicken — headed right for one another and then seeing who will swerve. And what's amazing is, they always manage to miss. I never saw two run into each other. The more I think about it, the more amazing these little creatures really seem to me. I need to find out more about them. So small, and so amazing.

Waterbugs skate....

FIGURE 4-1 Original Notebook Entry

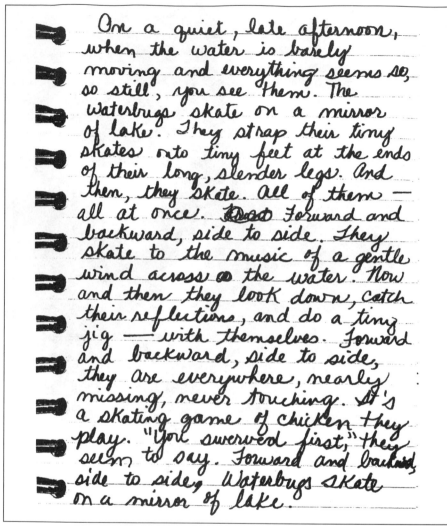

On a quiet, late afternoon, when the water is barely moving and everything seems so, so still, you see them. The waterbugs skate on a mirror of lake. They strap their tiny skates onto tiny feet at the ends of their long, slender legs. And then, they skate. All of them — all at once. ~~Does~~ Forward and backward, side to side. They skate to the music of a gentle wind across ~~so~~ the water. Now and then they look down, catch their reflections, and do a tiny jig — with themselves. Forward and backward, side to side, they are everywhere, nearly missing, never touching. It's a skating game of chicken they play. "You swerved first," they seem to say. Forward and backward, side to side, Waterbugs skate on a mirror of lake.

FIGURE 4–2 *Trying to Write Like Literature*

Curriculum Chunks

Here we are walking them through the actual focus of the strategy lesson: *try rewriting an existing entry and crafting it to sound like literature.*

Minilesson Text

is suited to trying this. Almost anything will do. It just needs to be something you just blurted out and weren't trying to write well at all, but you like what it says. It may be something like an entry that says, "Last night there was a full moon. It was very pretty. I could see it out my window. It was so bright I almost couldn't sleep . . . " You know, something you just kind of wrote down any old way. Find an entry like that.

Then you need to get the sound of some writing you like in your head—a sound you want to try and match. It could be anything—a Jane Yolen book, that *Hoops* (1997) book you all like so much. Anything. Feel free to pull the book and read some of it aloud before you start rewriting. And then just try it. Turn to a new page and start playing with the words from the original entry. So the one above you might start something like this, "A soft round moon floated across the sky, flooding my room with light. Bright light. White light. My own private night light." You know, something like that.

Okay. That's it. Could you raise your hand if you think this is a strategy you might want to try today during writing workshop? Who thinks this is something that makes sense for them? Maybe when we meet for share time then those of you who tried this can tell us how this strategy worked for you. Okay? Let's move out to our writing now and I hope you have a good day of it.

Sixteen different understandings and strategies are embedded in this teaching story in addition to the strategy that is the focus of the lesson. Whenever the embedded curriculum is spelled out like this, I am always struck by the fact that minilessons don't seem so mini after all. They seem like really big teaching. Now, we could choose any one of these understandings or strategies listed on the left side and turn it into the focus of the minilesson. If we chose a different focus for the lesson but used the same example, we would simply tell the story with the emphasis in a different place.

Even though we know there is so much important curriculum embedded in a single instance of teaching like this one, we still need to know, going in, what our focus is in the lesson. The focus keeps us from rambling and going on and on about things that don't matter as much. We can stay focused on one or two things if we have faith in the teaching embedded in the writing story to do its work.

Sample Minilesson on Finding Seed Ideas

Let's look at another lesson now from a different part of the process. In this lesson we are teaching students one way that writers find seed ideas for writing projects in their notebooks. Remember that a seed idea is the beginning move toward publication. Sometimes we know a lot about what kind of writing the finished piece will be, and sometimes we know very little, but a seed idea gets us moving in that direction as we begin work on a writing project.

The curricular focus of this minilesson is actually an understanding: *a seed idea can be a connection between several entries in the notebook written at very different times for different purposes.* This would be one of a series of minilessons designed to help students make better and better decisions about what writing projects to pursue out of all the ideas they've collected in their writers' notebooks. Again, notice the layers of teaching embedded in the lesson.

Curriculum Chunks

*Writers find seed ideas in their notebooks.

*Writers reread their notebooks.

*When rereading our notebooks, sometimes we find lines that ring true.

*Sometimes writers choose projects based on their interests.

*Writers have a good sense of what's in their notebooks.

*Try looking back through old notebooks to see what entries you already have that relate to your idea.

*Sometimes we have the start of something bigger already in our notebooks.

*Writers know themselves, their writing histories.

*Sometimes writers pursue projects to stretch themselves.

*Writers think about what work they need to do for a project.

*Writers do research.

*Sometimes we don't know at the outset what genre a writing project will become.

Minilesson Text

As we're thinking about all the different ways writers choose their seed ideas, I want to tell you about a seed idea I found in my notebook. Now, how I found this seed idea is really a two-part story. First, I was rereading entries and I came across this one about a dragonfly. It had this sentence in it: "There is this whole amazing world out there that, in its smallness, we miss so much of." That line sort of touched a chord in me because I really do believe this. I love to look at little tiny things in nature—insects, mushrooms, tiny flowers, single blades of grass. I am fascinated with their symmetry and beauty, and with how such little things are so sturdy. I began thinking that observing and writing about tiny things in nature could be a project I would enjoy working on.

The second part of this seed idea story is that I began to think, *I know I have a lot of entries in my notebooks already that come from observations of little things.* So I went back through my last two notebooks and found I had eleven such entries: two on gnats, two on spiders, two on water bugs, and one each on a lizard, a caterpillar, a dragonfly, two crows, and an inchworm. I realized that with these entries I had a good start already on this writing project.

I think that working on this project would stretch me as writer because I haven't done much writing about a topic like this—specific things in nature. I know if I worked on this I would want to observe more because I would want to base everything on firsthand observations.

I would also need to research the questions these tiny creatures pose for me.

At this point, I am unsure about what genre I would like to use. Poetry is one possibility, especially if I could do it

Curriculum Chunks

Writers think about different kinds of texts they know as they plan writing projects.

Any single seed idea could be written in a variety of ways.

Writers think about the future of their writing projects, especially their audiences.

Here we begin walking them through the actual focus of the lesson, the understanding: *a seed idea can be a connection between several entries in the notebook written at very different times for different purposes*

Minilesson Text

with nonfiction information to accompany it (sort of like *Cactus Poems* by Frank Asch and Ted Levin, 1998). Another possibility would be to write it as an informational text and take photographs to go with it—maybe even in second person like a Joanne Ryder book. I might even write it as a single, lyrical text that shows the beauty and wonder of tiny creatures—sort of like *Water Dance* by Thomas Locker (1997).

I am fascinated by this topic, I think it has real possibility as a writing project, and I would love to share my love of these creatures with others. I'm not sure of a specific audience, but I think I might gear it toward adults like me who are in danger of getting so busy that they miss seeing these amazing creatures.

Anyway, I have a lot of ideas about what I might do with this seed idea. The thing is, you might find that when you study your notebook for seed ideas, you actually find connections among a lot of different entries—like I did with all my entries about small creatures. You might read through your notebook and find you have lots of entries related to your grandmother's house or your big brother's soccer games or your feelings about the future. It could be anything. As long as it's a theme that runs across these different entries. As you are thinking today about this question (How can I make good seed idea decisions?), think about the connections among your entries. Are there some that go together around an idea that connects them? That could be your seed idea right there—the connections among several entries. If anyone finds a connection like this, be sure to let us know during share time today, okay? Have a good writing day.

Sample Minilesson on Nurturing a Seed Idea

This next minilesson is one in a series of lessons where we would be teaching students strategies for growing their seed ideas before they draft them. Remember that many teachers call this part of the writing process "nurturing," and because most inexperienced writers have never really done this before, they'll need us to show them a variety of ways to nurture their ideas. The curricular focus of this lesson is a strategy: *try making a list of questions about your seed idea and then using these questions as the focus for new entries.*

Curriculum Chunks

Writers use notebooks to find out what they need to say and to generate important material.

Writers use some strategies over and over.

Writers write different kinds of things.

Writers use notebooks purposefully, based on the work they're planning to do.

Sometimes writers force themselves to think in certain ways.

Sometimes in notebook entries writers just put everything they can think of down at first.

Minilesson Text

I know that all of you are beginning to work on better ways of growing your seed ideas in your writers' notebooks before drafting them. What we are trying to do is use this growing work in the notebook to help us become more focused on our seed ideas—to find out what things we really want to say about them and to help us generate some important material we can use for these ideas.

There's a strategy I use with basically any seed idea I am working on—from an idea for a fictional story to an idea for a poetry anthology on some topic to an idea for a persuasive essay on something I feel strongly about. This strategy helps me no matter what my idea is.

I go to some clean page in my notebook—I'll need a lot of space usually, and I just start asking questions about my topic. I sort of pretend like I've never really thought about this topic that much, and I just start asking questions like that kind of person—someone who has not thought much about this. Some of them are questions I've thought a lot about, and some are ones I've never really thought about. I'm just asking every one that comes to my mind—every one I can think of at first.

Curriculum Chunks	Minilesson Text
	Let me show you. One of the seed ideas I am working on is an editorial about what it means to be married—from my perspective at least. Here is the page in my notebook where I just wrote as many questions as I could think about related to marriage in my life [see Figure 4–3 on page 61].
Writers may have more than one writing project going at any time.	
	Notice that these are all related to my idea and that all of them are really "thinking" questions. I am trying to jumpstart my brain here. When I am writing these questions, I don't even worry about the answers. I just want good questions.
Writers sometimes ask questions to get their thinking going.	
	When I've got a pretty good list down and feel like I am running out, I begin the process of choosing one question at a time and writing an entry that thinks it through. That's what I was doing here—trying to think through the question, "How has my relationship with my family changed since I was married?" [see Figure 4–4 on page 62].
Sometimes we use writing to think something through.	*Note: We don't usually read all of a long entry like this. We read just enough for students to get a feel for what's happening in the writing.*
	Notice that I am just using the entry to think about this question. I'm not really trying to come to some final answer about it. Later, I reread entries like this one, entries where I am really thinking deeply about my idea, and highlight the places where I have said things about my idea that I think are really good. These become ways of saying things I could use in my draft.
Writers reread what they've written.	
Highlighters are good writing tools.	
Try searching entries for ways of saying things you might use in your draft.	
Seed ideas can lead to all kinds of writing.	So basically the strategy works like this: First, brainstorm a list of questions about your seed idea. They can be any kind of questions. If you're working with a story about something or someone, you might ask questions about one of the characters like, "What would make my character really afraid?" If you've got a more nonfictiony kind of topic, you might ask specific questions like, "Do birds have feelings?" and "Do birds think like members of families like we do?" If you've got a more memoir-like seed idea, you
Different kinds of writing require writers to think in different ways.	

How is my life different now as a married person?

Do people see me differently now — I mean those who used to know me when I was single?

What do other people who know us think about our marriage? Do they see us as happy?

What have I given up in this grand negotiation of marriage? What have I gained?

What would it be like to be single again — now after having been married?

Do I have more responsibilities now as a married person than I did when I was single?

How has my relationship with my family changed since I was married?

Is this the way I thought being married would be?

How do I envision my marriage in 10 years? In 50 years?

FIGURE 4–3 *Asking Questions About My Seed Idea*

How has my relationship with my family
changed since I've been married.

Well, it's changed a lot actually. Hannah
told me sometime ago that @y wasn't
as much fun since I got married. When
she first said it I felt this little crack
kind of in my heart. That part of me
that has this crazy need to be all things
to all people felt like a failure when
she said it. But then I had to stop for
a minute and think about what she was
saying. Things have changed a lot since
I've married and I think that in
the only way she knew how, she was
commenting on that. She's very
perceptive that way and I guess I
should really feel important in her
life to know it mattered enough to her
to notice—that things had really
changed. I mean, if she never noticed life
things were different at all, when

they are so different, then it should
worry me even more. Like she didn't
even care, do am I not fun anymore?
Well, they're stuff like I used to see
them a lot more. Before I met
Jim I went home more often and
they came here more often because
I didn't have a family of my own
outside of them (Jim) they hadn't
stopped being my family—I need
to think more about this, do we
don't see each other as often. Hannah
used to always sleep with me when
she spent the night and we'd
eat and play games and have
a great time. Now I have to put her
to bed by myself and it must feel a
little like living jilted I guess—like
Jim has taken her place. I used
to just play with her from morning

FIGURE 4-4 Thinking About One Question

guess. When the whole family was together I'd take the kids outside to play. Now I stay inside more where the adults are if Jim is there with me. I still take them for walks and do things, but it's not wild, unabandoned play we used to have. Of course some of that is because they have changed. They are growing up — Hannah 9 and Eric 13 and they don't play the same way they used to either. I guess the other big thing with them is that they rarely get me by themselves anymore. I come with Jim now, and they don't get all my attention anymore! But this is all only about Eric + Hannah. What about my relationships with Mom, Dad, Shauna + Andrew. I need to think about each of them separately next.

FIGURE 4–4 *continued*

might ask questions like, "Why is this memory sad for me?" or "What was I thinking when this happened?"

The point is, whatever the nature of your seed idea is, just start asking questions about it until you get a good working list down. Then you take questions, one at a time, write them at the top of a new notebook page and then write entries that get you thinking about each question. Write fast and long about these questions— capture everything that comes to mind. Later you can come back and use highlighters to capture the places where you really like your thinking.

So if you are stuck for a way to grow your seed idea to- day, try using this questioning strategy as a way to gen- erate some good notebook writing around your seed. We'll see who tried it during share time.

Sample Minilessons on Revision

This next minilesson would come near the end of a series of minilessons focused on revision strategies and understandings. Revision can actually be a very interesting part of the process for students if we teach them to see it as a chance to play around with what's possible in a draft instead of making them think they have to revise because they didn't do it right the first time. We need to show students specific things that writers do and try and think about during revision so that they de- velop a repertoire of ways to engage in this part of the process. In this minilesson we are teaching a strategy for revision: *try reading a touchstone text by a writing mentor to get revision ideas for a draft.*

Thinking It Through...

This may be a good time to stop and think about what you are noticing about these minilesson examples. What strikes you about the teaching? What perplexes you? If you are studying with others, talk together about what you're noticing. You might want to develop some theories about the teaching that you can test out in these next lessons.

Curriculum Chunks

Writers use some of the strategies for revision again and again.

Revision is meant to make the writing the best that it can be.

Writers have other authors as mentors and texts they know and love.

Writers make "moves" when they craft a text.

Writers try things in drafts.

Touchstone texts don't have to be written in the same genre to help writers with their revisions.

Writers make things sound good with words, sentences, and parts of texts.

Writers use their notebooks to play around and try rewriting things in their drafts.

Writers think about what their readers' reactions will be.

Minilesson Text

Today I want to talk to you about something I often do with my drafts when I am in the last stages of my revisions. When I'm feeling like I've almost done all I can do to a piece of writing to make it the best it can be, I like to spend some time looking at particular texts by particular authors I really love. I call these my touchstone texts by my mentor authors. I take my draft, and I go sit down with one of these books, and I ask myself, "What moves with words, sentences, punctuation, etc. has this writer made here that might work well in my text?" Basically, I'm just trying to see if there is anything in my touchstone text I might want to try in my own draft.

This is a little complicated, so let me tell you about doing it here just recently. With my editorial I've shown you before about being independently married, I decided to sit my draft alongside Cynthia Rylant's *Scarecrow* (1998) and see if there was anything I might try. Now, I know that *Scarecrow* is a *very* different kind of writing than my editorial, but that didn't really matter to me. I wasn't looking at what it was about, I was just looking at how she used words and sentences and parts of the text to make it sound so good. I wanted to see if there was anything I might try in my draft.

I actually found several things that I played around with in my notebook, rewriting parts of my draft using the same craft that she used, but let me just tell you about one, to help you see what I mean.

I loved that part in *Scarecrow* where she tells you that the scarecrow needs to have a friendliness toward birds. And then you turn the page and she writes, "Yes, birds." It's like she knows you as the reader are going to be thinking, *Birds?? But scarecrows are supposed to scare birds away, not be friendly!* She knows the reader is wondering *what's up?* so she just kind of speaks directly to the

Sample Minilesson on Nurturing a Seed Idea ◆ 65

Writers can speak directly to their readers' responses in their texts.

reader and answers the question she knows is in his or her head. "Yes, birds." It makes the text feel almost intimate, like the narrator is really trying very hard to communicate with the reader.

Well, I loved this part of her text, but I also realized I had a part in my draft where speaking to the reader in that way might work. At least two people had read my draft and both of them expressed astonishment at this one spot. You remember yesterday I showed you this part of my draft where one long paragraph ends and is followed by a one-sentence paragraph? Well, look at what follows it in the very next paragraph: ". . . and I knew, I just knew, that life was more than okay, life was good. I realized at that moment, that I didn't need to be married.

Writers let other people read their drafts while they are still working on them.

It wasn't a decision; it was just a realization.

The next week, I met Jim. A year and a half later I married him. Not because I needed to, because I wanted to . . ."

This was the part where both my readers seemed so surprised. As a matter of fact, they both said, "You met him the *next week*?" So, I decided that I could do what Rylant was doing in *Scarecrow*; I could insert an answer to the question I know most of my readers are going to have. So I simply rewrote it and added:

Writers pay attention and remember their readers' responses.

Writers rewrite.

Writers add things to drafts.

"The next week, I met Jim. That's right, the very next week. A year and a half later I married him. Not because I needed to, because I wanted to . . ."

Writers think about how their texts will work with readers.

I think this adds a lot to my text, letting me have that same kind of intimate contact with my reader that Rylant has.

Curriculum Chunks	Minilesson Text
Here we are walking students through the actual focus of the lesson, a strategy: *try reading a touchstone text by a writing mentor to get revision ideas for a draft.* *Sometimes writers try things during revision that they decide not to use in their final drafts.*	If any of you feel like you are getting burned out with this whole revision process, you might try what I tried with my draft. Find one or two touchstone texts, books or articles that you really love, and sit them alongside your drafts. Ask yourselves, "What craft moves has this writer made in this book that might work well in my text?" And the "moves" can be anything—stuff the writer is doing with words, sentences, punctuation, structure. Anything. If you see something you'd like to try in your draft, have a go at it in your notebook first, and then if you like it, you can insert it in your final drafts. Let the writers you really admire give you some ideas for things to try in your drafts. Okay? We'll talk about this during share time today.

Because revision is one of the most challenging parts of the writing process for us as teachers, we're going to look at one more lesson on revision that works a little differently from the first one. In this lesson, we start out by defining for students one of the most common bits of writing advice we know, *"show, don't tell."* In this lesson, we take this advice and teach students how to use it as a strategic tool for revision: *search your draft for any places where you might be telling something that needs to be shown. Rewrite it so that you show, don't tell.* Notice that this lesson is from the same draft of writing used in the preceding minilesson. This is very common. We can get a lot of teaching mileage from a single writing experience once we learn to think specifically about the curriculum embedded in the experience.

> ### Thinking It Through...
> Before you read this last minilesson, you may want to fold some paper and cover up the left column. As you read through (by yourself or with someone else), try and name the curriculum chunks you see embedded in the lesson.

Curriculum Chunks	Minilesson Text

Curriculum Chunks

*Writers commonly fall into writing "traps."

*Writers draft with readers in mind.

*Writing well helps readers form understandings.

*Writers have things they always check for during revision of any draft.

*Writers reread their drafts looking for specific things.

*Writers rewrite.

*Sometimes writers use their notebooks to try out rewrites.

*Writers revise with readers in mind.

Minilesson Text

This morning I'd like to teach you something to look for as you are working on revising your drafts. One of the most common traps writers fall into is they try and *tell* things in their drafts instead of *showing* them. They say things like, "The little boy was very angry." Well, that's telling me something, not showing me. If you want to make writing come to life for your readers, you have to *show* them he's angry. So instead of writing, "The little boy was very angry," you might write it like this:

"The little boy spontaneously balled his fists into tight little bullets, clutched at his side. You could see the red rising slowing from the bottom of his face to the top. And when he spoke, it was more of a hissing than a regular voice."

Now, that makes the reader think, "My, this little boy is angry." Write it so the reader can see it, and then you don't even have to say, "he's angry." The reader will just know.

One revision check I always make of any draft is to see if there are any places where I am telling instead of showing. I read through, and if I see a place like this, I underline the telling part, and then I lift that part out and rewrite it so that it shows. Sometimes I do this right in the draft, and sometimes I do it in my notebook first and then insert the rewrite into the draft.

Let me show you an example. In my editorial about being married, I realized I was telling my reader something in this part right here:

"I mean, I was busy. Busy doing what needed to be done to find a life for myself. Busy becoming *extremely independent.*"

I realized that by telling that in this big way—extremely independent—my readers might not even know how I was defining that and so wouldn't really know what I meant. I decided to rewrite that part so that it *showed* this better. Here's my rewrite:

Writers rewrite.

"I mean, I was busy. Busy doing what needed to be done to find a life for myself. And I remember the moment, the exact moment when I was thirty-one years old, that I sat on the front porch of the new house I had just bought for myself, I let my fingers play with the curly hair I had decided to stop straightening, I sipped coffee from a mug one of my students had given me that said, 'Teachers can change the world,' and I knew, I just knew, that life was more than okay, life was good. I realized at that moment that I didn't need to be married.

Writers can stretch ideas out.

It wasn't a decision; it was simply a realization."

This is me stretching that idea of being independent out and trying to show this without ever having to actually tell it. The idea that life was good, even if I was living it all by myself, was my way of showing this—along with some other little details slipped in like the house and the hair-straightening decision. I actually worked on this awhile in my notebook before I came up with the showing I liked.

Sometimes writers have to try a rewrite several ways before they are happy with it.

Writers can help each other.

Here we are walking them through the actual focus of the lesson, a strategy: *search your draft for any places where you might be telling something that needs to be shown. Rewrite it so that you show, don't tell.*

I'd like for you all to take a little of workshop time today to help each other search your drafts to see if there are places where you have told things, really big things, that really need to be *shown* instead. Maybe you've written something like "My grandmother is very <u>nice</u>" or "Sasha, my dog, is lots of <u>fun</u>." Take these big "code word" adjectives like *nice* and *fun* and try rewriting them so the reader is the one who says, "Man, your grandmother is really *nice*." Write it more like this, "Every day when she picks me up from school, she has a candy bar sitting on my seat just for me. She knows all my favorite kinds, and

Minilesson Text

always makes sure she buys them . . ." Write a little section of text that *shows* us what you are trying to tell us.

You can use your writers' notebooks as toolboxes for these revisions if you'd like. Try the rewrite in your notebook first until it's ready to insert in your draft. During share time later, let's look at some of the rewrites you did to change any telling parts to showing. Okay?

As I study a collection of minilessons like these, two main things strike me. First, I notice that many of the same curricular themes come up over and over again in very different lessons. When I see this, I am reminded of the power of teaching and learning *over time*. The most essential curriculum of process is not taught in single minilessons, or even two or three lessons. The curriculum is woven into the very fabric of every story we tell, every example we give, and every interaction we have with students around writing in our classrooms. Over time, we come to trust this talk that shapes our teaching.

Second, as I read through minilessons like these, I am always struck by how predictably patterned they are. The lessons almost always start by situating the lesson in the ongoing work of the students' writing, letting them know how the lesson is meant to support that work. Next, there is the storytelling part where the teacher actually walks students through a writing experience ending with the focus of the lesson. Before students are sent out to work, the teacher explicitly states the content of the lesson, untied from the writing story example, and then helps students envision thinking this or doing this in their own writing work. And each lesson ends with either an invitation or a requirement for students to try the lesson out in their independent writing work.

When our minilessons have a predictable pattern to them, a sort of teaching rhythm that students recognize, I believe it helps students better attend to the teaching. They know what to expect from lessons like these and so they can focus very clearly on the content instead of having to figure out the bigger picture of what's happening in the lesson. The pattern we've outlined here is surely not the only effective one, but whatever way of teaching process lessons we find, we need to keep them simple, focused, and routine.

References

Asch, Frank, and Ted Levin. 1998. *Cactus Poems*. New York: A Gulliver Green Book, Harcourt Brace.

Burleigh, Robert. 1997. *Hoops*. New York: Silver Whistle, Harcourt Brace.

Locker, Thomas. 1997. *Water Dance*. New York: Harcourt Brace.

Paulsen, Gary. 1999. *Canoe Days*. Illustrated by Ruth Wright Paulsen. New York: Bantam Doubleday Dell Publishing Group.

Rylant, Cynthia. 1998. *Scarecrow*. Illustrated by Lauren Stringer. New York: Harcourt Brace.

CHAPTER 5

Letting Authors Co-Teach the Curriculum of Process

When professional authors talk, teachers of writing listen. We really listen because we know that embedded in what they say is important process curriculum we can lay alongside our own understandings and strategies. Throughout the book so far, we've made references to letting professional authors "co-teach" the process of writing with us. Now, we want to slow that down just a little and make sure we're clear on how that happens in our curriculum development. We won't have to stay here long, however, because we'll be using all the same lines of thinking we've been using to look at our own writing experiences.

When we see finished pieces of published writing—picture books, novels, feature articles, poems—we can't see the process that came behind them. We can think about what the process might have been, and that's useful thinking for developing writers, but it's not as rich as when professional authors step out from behind their texts and tell us a little about how they do what they do. We attend the professional author sessions at conferences, we read interviews with authors, we watch the Book TV channel and mark Oprah's Book Club day on our calendars, and we invite authors to speak in our classrooms. We scour author's notes and book flaps and websites for any insights they might offer into how authors do what they do. And just as we write like teachers of writing, we listen like teachers of writing to what professional authors say about their processes.

We listen and then we make the same curricular move we make as we study our own writing. We move from the specifics in what authors say to more general understandings and strategies we can teach our students. We are searching for the answers to the same guiding questions we ask of our own writing:

> What kinds of things do writers think about and why do they think about these things?

> What kinds of things do writers do and how and why do they do them?

To illustrate this curricular move, let's take this quote from Virginia Hamilton on Scholastic's website. The interviewer asked Virginia where she got the idea for *Plain City*. Her response:

> I was teaching at Ohio State University and I got caught in a winter ice storm. I pulled off the interstate onto the off ramp. The sign said "Plain City." There was also a McDonald's sign, and I decided to pull off and wait until the storm was over. I did that, but I never found the "Mickey D's" and I never found Plain City—I drove about six miles! After that, every time I drove down that road I'd pass that sign and I'd wonder about Plain City. Then I started making up what the town would be like, and the people, and that's how I made up Buhlaire and all the other characters. You know, I still have never been to Plain City. I'm kind of afraid to go now. But I have heard that it is kind of like what I made up. In fact, they have a river, and it does flood!

As we read this, we can see clearly one of the essential curricular understandings we've already established—that Virginia Hamilton gets ideas away from her desk. But because she tells a little about her thinking and what she did as a writer, we can dig out even more curriculum from this quote:

◆ *Sometimes a writing idea comes from something you wonder about over and over (an understanding).*
◆ *If there is a place you have always wondered about, try making up characters and a setting to go with that place to help satisfy your wonder and give you writing ideas (a strategy).*
◆ *Sometimes writers become very attached to the stories they create and the fictional world becomes almost real to them (an understanding).*

The last understanding is an interpretation based on her fear of going and seeing the real town. We could take any one of these chunks of curriculum and embed it in a series of minilessons with a common focus. We might use Virginia Hamilton's writing life as the example in the lesson all by itself, or we could combine it with examples from our own writing lives or even examples from other professional authors. We could, of course, also share any of these understandings or this strategy with a student in a writing conference.

The key to developing curriculum from what professional authors say is to make that same move we've been making (with our own writing) from the specifics in their stories to the general statements that help us envision possibilities for our students. We are always thinking into the future of our students' lives, *what difference might it make if my students understood this or tried this?* The *this*, of course, is what Virginia Hamilton or any other professional author understands and does. These generalizations that we ferret out of what writers say become very specific things we can teach our students.

To illustrate this kind of thinking even further, we'll take a look at the curriculum I found from one experience hearing an author talk about her work. Robin Epstein is a writer of feature articles and editorials, and she graciously came to speak to my class once as we were studying this kind of writing. As

Robin talked, I made many notes and later I returned to those notes and studied them as a teacher of writing. I asked myself, "What is there to know about writing from what Robin told us?" In the table that follows, I made note of what Robin said on the left side, and on the right side I have stated the more general curriculum I see in what she said.

What Robin Told Us	Curriculum Statement
The idea for her piece "Dirty Air Fund" came from a conversation she had with a friend. The friend actually said, "We need a dirty air fund!" The words her friend said put her on this journey of thought.	You might capture phrases you hear that you think would work well in your writing. You can use *exact* words someone says to get the language you need for your writing.
When Robin wants to publish in a specific publication, she reads to see what kind of writing that publication likes to publish and what kinds of topics seem to "fit" there. She uses what she learns from this inquiry to help her decide on a topic and on how to write it.	If you know where you want to be published, you might spend time "reading around" that publication to see how others have been successful at that and to get a vision for how you should write.
Robin says that she reads novels very fast—races through them. Newspapers she reads very, very slowly.	When you know you are a certain kind of writer, you might read the *kind* of writing you do differently from other kinds of writing.
Robin pointed out that on the Op Ed page of the newspaper, the writer's picture appears with the piece. She said this has to do with the fact that the voice of the piece is so important. This type of writing is supposed to be voice driven. She feels her voice is strongest in these pieces.	Writers might ask themselves, "What have I done to the writing (punctuation, word choice, sentence structure, etc.) to give it voice?"

What Robin Told Us

Robin said in a piece she was doing for a New York City paper, it was important to mention all the boroughs of the city as she gave examples. She had to do some research to accomplish this—she needed specific information on each one.

When using items or sentences in a series, Robin thinks about how many is the right number to have. There is no magical right number, she says, you just kind of have to feel whether it is too many, too few, or just enough.

As Robin noticed something in her draft that might be confusing to her reader (real animals versus fake animals), she thought that one way to fix it would be to capitalize the names of real animals.

Robin says that her research often drives how a piece of writing will be divided into sections. She organizes her research notes into sections, and these become sections of the draft.

Robin tells us about a man she worked with at a newspaper who was given a column to write. She says she didn't know he even had opinions! He had to get some to write his column.

When Robin is trying to get her words to work in a certain way in a text (with something like alliteration) and

Curriculum Statement

You might think about your audience as you make decisions about what details and examples to include in a piece to illustrate or support your point. "Name dropping" can help you connect with that audience.

You might look for places where you are listing several things together. Ask yourself this question, "How many of these do I really need here? Does my list feel right?"

Sometimes you don't need more words to make something clear. Sometimes you can manipulate print or punctuation to make something clearer.

One way to begin to structure how a draft will go is to organize your research notes and notebook writing and see what sections naturally emerge from that.

If you know you are going to be doing a certain kind of writing, then you might have to "get a life" that helps you find material for that writing.

If you are feeling stuck because you can't think of a word you need somewhere, you can just leave a blank and keep drafting. You can come back to it later.

What Robin Told Us	Curriculum Statement
she can think of some words she needs but not others, she will leave a blank and keep writing and come back to it later.	
Robin wrote a review of the same movie for two very different kinds of publications: The Nation and Vogue. Her slant on the movie was quite different based on the audiences for the two pieces.	There are lots of ways to write about the same topic. One of the things that can influence *how* we write something is what we think the audience would be interested in— what they want to hear about.

The strategies and understandings on the right can now be the content for minilessons or writing conferences. Notice that if you only read the right side, Robin is totally absent. Her stories as an author have become curriculum, un-tied from her context. If we teach a lesson with some chunk of this content as the focus, we would tell students about Robin as an author and then share with them what she said that leads us to the specific thing we want to teach them in the lesson. Sometimes it will make sense to show them the piece of writing that corresponds with what she has said, as it might in the lesson using "Dirty Air Fund" as the example, or the piece that has the distinction between fake animals and real animals. Often, however, what authors say about their processes

> ### *Thinking It Through…*
>
> *Once again, you might think about any writing experiences you've had that led you to understandings or strategies similar to Robin's. Can you imagine teaching lessons from your own experiences— maybe combining your story with hers as an example?*

aren't tied to specific pieces of writing and so this isn't necessary. We simply quote the author and help students make the curriculum move to understanding the focus of the lesson in their own writing work.

Notice, also, that the strategies and understandings on the right side of this column are stated more as possibilities than as facts or truths: "you might try this . . ." or "one way to . . ." We must state the curriculum this way because we know that what we learn from any one author represents just one way to go about the process of writing.

Finding Connections and *Disconnections*

As we bring our co-teachers of writing in to help us develop the curriculum of process, one thing will become apparent fairly quickly: *there is no single, right, and magical process for writing.* If you ask fifty different writers the same question about their writing, you might very well get fifty different answers. Some of them will be variations of the same answer (connections), but some of them will just be outright different ways of thinking about writing or going about writing (disconnections).

Thinking It Through...

If you are reading this book with a study group, you might first try having everyone write a response to some specific question about the process of writing. Then talk to compare all your responses. Think about what you might learn from the connections and disconnections you find in your own processes. Listen carefully as people explain, you might want to use them as examples with your students someday!

To illustrate what we mean, we can look at Jeffrey and Vicky Copeland's collection of interviews with poets, *Speaking of Poets 2* (1994, NCTE). This book is a treasure trove for curriculum development because the interviewers ask the authors many of the same questions. Let's just look at what a few of the authors say about the physical act of getting the words down on paper for the first time:

J. Patrick Lewis: "There was a time when I wrote longhand on yellow legal pads and swore I'd never use a word processor, but now I can't imagine going back to legal pads. A computer is so writer-friendly. For me, there is just something about being able to juggle words around and printing a poem right away" (5).

Cynthia Rylant: "I never use machines. You'll never see me sitting at a typewriter or writing on a word processor while I'm composing . . . When I first started writing, I wrote with an ink pen on yellow legal pads because it was cheap . . . I have never changed from that method . . . I don't get to the type-writer until everything is finished in longhand and polished. The only reason I use a typewriter is so I can send it in to the publisher" (25).

Jane Yolen: "Most of the time I need to be working on the typewriter. I don't use a computer, even though my husband is a professor of computer science. I use a typewriter because I can't write poetry in longhand. For some reason I need to see what it looks like in print" (80).

Victor Martinez: "One superstition I have involves the pens and pencils I use to write poems. If I'm out for a walk and find a pen or pencil on the street, I pick it up, bring it home, and write with it . . . I always try to imagine who owned it, how they lost it, and what is going on for them in life. It may sound strange, but I really feel I get something from these pens and pencils. To me, it is almost as if through these pens I get to see into another person's soul" (162).

So what, exactly, should we teach students about getting those drafts down on paper? Word processors? Longhand? Typewriters? Magically found pens and pencils? The "right" answer about what we should teach is all these an-swers. We teach all of these as possibilities. We start with a curricular understanding that is larger than any one of these answers from professional authors: *writers find ways that work best for them to get drafts down on paper.* Then, using different options from professional authors, our own writing experiences, and the experiences of our students as examples, we teach a series of minilessons that show students different possibilities for how to begin work on drafts. The goal of this teaching is for students to find ways of working for themselves.

Thinking It Through...

Study groups might take the question they just answered (or another one) and have everyone go in search of a quote from a professional author that is a response to the question. Again, as you discuss, you can look for connections and disconnections and examples you might use in your teaching.

We find this same variety of author responses to questions about most any aspect of writing. This is per-haps the most fundamental curriculum knowledge of all about the process—that it can happen in different ways at different times for different writers. We tend not to like things like this in schools, things that can go any number of ways. Sometimes things like this make us want to throw our hands up and say, "Why teach anything if you can do it any way you like?" More than one road to a common outcome makes our teaching more challenging, but to simplify it and make everyone do everything the same way is to change the very nature of the thing we are trying to teach. It helps if we stay focused on those larger curricular understandings like the one just mentioned: *writers find ways that work best for them to get drafts down on paper.* Staying focused on these larger understandings helps us remember we *do* have something specific we are trying to teach, even as we are presenting students with a number of options for how they might accomplish whatever it is.

My friend Isoke Nia often takes quotes from professional authors about some aspect of the writing process, copies them for students, and then asks students to find an author whose process most closely matches their own. They then have rich conversations about the connections and disconnections they find between their own writing and the writing of professional authors. Naming the ways they work best also helps students begin to form partnerships with other writers who work in similar ways, and to seek out those who work differently so they can learn other ways of going through the process.

As teachers of writing, we start with what we know from our own writing experiences as a sort of baseline of curriculum knowledge, but then we use our co-teachers of writing to deepen and expand what we know. As we study what our co-teachers say, we are on the lookout for things we might never think about or do ourselves but that we think might be interesting to a group of developing writers who are trying out all sorts of possibilities for getting their writing work done. Filling a classroom up with possibilities for how this work might go is really at the heart of teaching writing, both with process and with products, as we'll see in later chapters.

We are reading interviews and listening to what writers say in search of possibilities. For example, when reading the book *Author Talk*, another treasure trove for curriculum development compiled by Leonard S. Marcus, I was so taken with what Johanna Hurwitz said in response to a question about what she does when she is stuck. She says, "When I was having trouble making progress with *Spring Break* (1997), I decided as a kind of experiment to start with the last chapter and write the book backward. To my delight, it worked. But I don't plan to write all my books backward" (46).

I was fascinated by this as a two-part chunk of curriculum: *if you are stuck in a draft, you might try writing the ending and working backward through the draft* (a strategy). And, *writers don't always use the same drafting process for every piece of writing* (an understanding). I already knew that second part from my own writing experience, but I have never tried writing something backward. I have, however, known students who might find this a very interesting thing to try.

One good way to organize quotes from authors as curriculum is to make a database (either on the computer or on good, old-fashioned note cards) of quotes and the curriculum chunks we might teach from them. We then can file them according to the various writing issues they address. Groups of teachers working together on curriculum development can share good quotes and expand their files much more quickly.

Rather than listing a bibliography for good sources of author quotes like these, I'll share a few examples from my own co-teaching file and let the citations (only one from each source) on each serve as a bibliography for a few good resources. I have chosen to include here only those sources that interview or survey a variety of authors because these books give you the most mileage if you are just getting started. A variety of authors' voices helps us show students that there are many ways to go about the writing process. But it bears saying that many books about just one author's writing life and process are full of wonderful curriculum as well. Also, we can get

> ### Thinking It Through...
>
> You might want to find an interview with a writer and go on a curriculum "dig" to see what you can find in what the author says. Remember to look for comments that answer our two essential questions: What kinds of things do writers think about and why do they think about these things? *and* What kinds of things do writers do and how and why do they do them?

great quotes from listening to authors speak at conferences or on radio or TV, from the author's notes in books, and sometimes from statements on book jackets.

I have the quote on one side of each curriculum card and the curriculum spelled out on the other. The underlined heading on the curriculum side indicates the larger writing issue the curriculum addresses. We can organize series of minilessons around these larger issues. In each minilesson, we tell a little about the author, share the quote, and then help students make the curricular connection that is the focus of the lesson.

Writers' Work Habits

If you are having trouble finishing projects, you might want to set deadlines and work toward them.

Back

Gary Soto:

"I also try to put time lines on what I do. I'm actually quite antsy about completing projects. Sometimes I admit this doesn't make for the best writing, but that's my writing habit. My writings occur because I do use deadlines. Otherwise, I would procrastinate away. After I set this deadline, I work consistently until I wrap it up."

J. S. Copeland. 1993. *Speaking of Poets.* Urbana, IL: NCTE, p. 93.

Front

Living in the World as a Writer

Take your notebook somewhere interesting and gather notes as a writer.

POETRY

Poems can grow from observational notes.

Back

Patricia Hubbell:

"I went to a Little League baseball game and took lots of notes about what was going on. I sat in the bleachers and watched the crowd and what was happening all around me. I can still remember how a foul ball went out of the park and hit a car. Then I went home and wrote the poem. Last summer I went to about twenty agricultural fairs and took several notebooks full of notes. Then I came back and wrote poems from the notes and from what I'd remembered and thought about."

J. S. and V. L. Copeland. 1994. *Speaking of Poets 2*. Urbana, IL: NCTE, p. 154.

Front

Growing a Seed Idea

Try asking yourself "what if" questions about your seed idea.

Back

James Howe:

"I start [a book] with an idea I've jotted down in a notebook. I have file folders full of ideas. If the idea catches fire, I'll develop it by writing in longhand whatever occurs to me—just letting my mind float. I ask myself lots of 'what if?' questions: *What if the rabbit attacks vegetables instead of people? What if the girl is painfully shy? What if she's shy because she's afraid of something? What might she be afraid of?* At some point I know I've done enough of what I call 'prewriting' and realize it's time to start writing the story."

L. S. Marcus, ed. 2000. *Author Talk*. New York: Simon & Schuster, pp. 39–40.

Front

Fiction—Drafting

As your plot is developing, try asking these two questions: "What will the reader expect to have happen right now?" and "What totally unexpected thing can I have happen instead?" Be sure that what you choose is believable.

Back

Kristi Holl:

"At each turn in the plot I ask myself two questions: 'What will the reader expect to have happen right now?' and 'What totally unexpected thing can I have happen instead?' Whatever I choose has to be believable, though. Otherwise the reader will stop reading. I don't choose a bizarre twist of circumstances unless I can make it believable."

S. Asher, ed. 1996. *But That's Another Story*. New York: Walker and Company, p. 56.

Front

Drafting and Revision

It's okay if things don't come out the way you want them to at first. Just keep writing, even if it's not very good. You can rewrite.

Back

Toni Morrison:

"When you first start writing—and I think it's true for a lot of beginning writers—you're scared to death that if you don't get that sentence right that minute it's never going to show up again. And it isn't. But it doesn't matter—another one will, and it'll probably be better. And I don't mind writing badly for a couple of days because I know I can fix it—and fix it again and again, and it will be better . . . I rewrite a lot, over and over again, so that it looks like I never did."

W. Zinsser, ed. 1987. *Inventing the Truth: The Art and Craft of Memoir*. Boston: Houghton Mifflin, pp. 122–123.

Front

Living a Writing Life—Notebooks

One thing you can collect in your writer's notebook are quotes that interest you.

Back

Naomi Shihab Nye:

"I have also kept notebooks of things *other* people say—even people I don't know, in airports, on trains. Students in lunch lines at school. Sometimes these quotes are very mysterious, or intriguing, and will lead us somewhere else. I have a whole notebook filled with quotes by an old friend of mine named Kerry, one of the best talkers I ever knew. When we have difficulty thinking of a beginning for a piece of writing, we . . . might do better to start with a line we have heard, letting it be an invitation into the piece."

R. Fletcher. 1996. *A Writer's Notebook.* New York: Avon Books, pp. 66–67.

Front

Drafting and Revision

Writers sometimes do things with language on purpose to make something they write work a certain way.

Back

Gary Paulsen:

"Language, really, is a dance for me. I long ago decided that I would do anything possible to make a story work right—including sometimes getting fast and loose with grammar. Story is all, and language is a tool to make the story work right and should, I think, be kept flexible to fit needs."

A. A. McClure and J. V. Kristo. 1996. *Books That Invite Talk, Wonder, and Play.* Urbana, IL: NCTE, p. 276.

Front

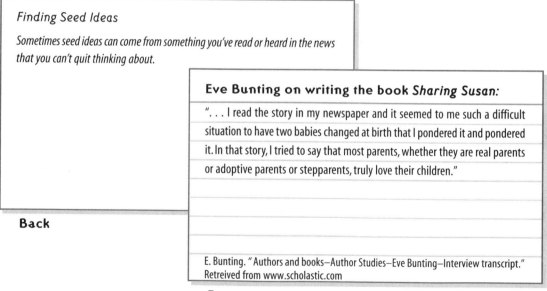

Drafting and Revision

As you draft and revise, try to hear the words you're writing as if they were being read aloud (you might even want to read them aloud). If they don't sound right to you, work on them until they do.

Back

C.S. Lewis:

"Always write (and read) with the ear, not the eye. You should hear every sentence you write as if it was being read aloud or spoken."

D. M. Murray. 1990. *Shoptalk: Learning to Write with Writers*. Portsmouth, NH: Boynton/Cook, p. 134.

Front

Finding Seed Ideas

Sometimes seed ideas can come from something you've read or heard in the news that you can't quit thinking about.

Back

Eve Bunting on writing the book *Sharing Susan:*

". . . I read the story in my newspaper and it seemed to me such a difficult situation to have two babies changed at birth that I pondered it and pondered it. In that story, I tried to say that most parents, whether they are real parents or adoptive parents or stepparents, truly love their children."

E. Bunting. "Authors and books—Author Studies—Eve Bunting—Interview transcript." Retreived from www.scholastic.com

Front

Drafting and Revision

Try writing your draft using any words you can think of. Just get it down, then go back and cut out all the parts that aren't necessary.

NONFICTION

When revising nonfiction, check your facts over and over.

Back

Ilene Cooper on writing *The Dead Sea Scrolls*:

"When it finally came time to write, with so many complicated aspects to the narrative, the word I had to keep reminding myself of was *simplify*. First, I'd write a part of the text, for instance the discovery of the scrolls in the cave. I'd use any words I wanted and write it as long as I thought it should be. Then, I'd start to cut. I'd whittle away any part of the narrative that wasn't interesting or necessary. After that, I'd work on each paragraph, paring it down, tightening sentences, making sure I was using just the right word . . . then it was time to go back and check every fact in each sentence. That I did over and over again."

I. Cooper. May 1997. "The Inside Story." *Book Links*. American Library Association, p. 17.

Front

References

Copeland, Jeffrey S., and Vicky L. Copeland. 1994. *Speaking of Poets 2: More Interviews with Poets Who Wrote for Children and Young Adults*. Orbana, IL: NCTE.

Hamilton, Virginia. "Authors and Books–Author Studies–Virginia Hamilton–Interview Transcript." Retrieved from www.scholastic.com

Marcus, L.S., ed. 2000. *Author Talk*. New York: Simon & Schuster.

CHAPTER 6

Read Like a Teacher of Writing

I am sitting in the kitchen having breakfast and looking at the morning paper. There's an editorial by one of my favorite syndicated writers, Leonard Pitts of the *Miami Herald*. In our local paper the piece has been titled, "Offended by the News Media? We're So Sorry!" The piece is about the chairman of Viacom Inc., Sumner Redstone's admonition to members of the news media to take more care to report the news without being "unnecessarily offensive to foreign governments." About a third of the way through the piece Pitts states that he's decided Redstone has a point. Pitts writes:

> Think of all the times news media have reported on desperate Cubans sailing away on inner tubes to escape that prison island, all the times we've described the hunger, poverty and incidental cruelties of life in that nation. Yet we never once stopped to think how this might make Castro feel. How thoughtless we were. Soulless dictators are human, too. (Pitts 1999, A7)

As the piece continues, it becomes increasingly clear that Pitts is actually making an argument that is clearly opposite from what he really believes. By the end of the piece, he has, sarcastically, apologized for possible offenses to everyone from human rights violators to drunk drivers to child molesters to Charles Manson.

I get up in the middle of my breakfast and go and get the scissors. I have to show this my students, I think. This is such an interesting way to pose an argument—as if you actually agree with the opposing side . . .

* * *

In Part One of this book, we explored what it means to write like teachers of writing. To write like the kinds of people we are so that we have curriculum knowledge about the *process* of writing that runs true and deep in our teaching. Now we want to take that same idea and think about it with reading. How do teachers of writing *read* so that they develop curriculum knowledge about the products of writing? Whenever I think about this question, I always think about Mara.

Mara, a first-grade teacher, was driving along a winding rural road once after a lunch out with friends. She was chatting away with the two of them who had hitched rides with her when, suddenly, in the middle of the conversation, she slammed on the brakes and pulled to the roadside. Mara jumped out of the car without a word, her two friends gaping. She went behind the car and disappeared just a little ways down an embankment, then came back up pulling a huge, appliance-sized empty box behind her. She lifted the back of her SUV, slid the box in, slammed it closed, jumped back in the driver's seat, put it in gear, and finished the sentence she had left undone before all this happened. When finally someone else could get a word in, she asked, "Uh, Mara. What are you going to do with that box?"

"I don't know," Mara said. "I'll take it to school. The kids will figure out something interesting to do with it."

Mara *drives* through the world like a first-grade teacher. She is constantly on the lookout for things that have potential. Often, she doesn't even know what that potential might be exactly, but she knows her students well enough and she understands what she wants for them deeply enough to recognize potential when she sees it. So she stops whatever she is doing and gathers it and then can't wait for the day she can take it into her classroom and see what her students will make of it.

I think this is what it means to read like teachers of writing.

We read like Mara drives.

The world is full of writing that makes us slam on our brakes when we're reading and think, *Ooo . . . look at that. I need to show that to my students. That's really good writing.* That's what happened that morning as I read Leonard Pitts' editorial and left my breakfast to go get the scissors. I wasn't any more thinking about teaching that morning than Mara was out driving with friends. I was just having breakfast and reading the morning paper. But I can't help it, I read like a teacher of writing. That's who I am. And when I happen upon some really good stuff, I have to gather it for my teaching.

Magazines, newspapers, memos, novels, billboards, email messages, lyrics, letters, poems, short stories. Every time we see writing, we are seeing what we teach. We are seeing examples of what's possible in writing, and so we have to read the texts we encounter across our lives differently than other people. We read these texts like teachers of writing. We are on the lookout for interesting ways to approach the writing, interesting ways to craft sentences and paragraphs and whole texts, interesting ways to bring characters to life or make time move or get a point across. When we read, we are always on the lookout—whether we intend to be or not—for interesting things we might teach our students how to do.

Thinking It Through...

Think about your reading life. You probably don't need to get a different one. You just need to learn to read a little differently inside the reading life you already have. What kinds of things do you read on a regular basis? Make a list of your "regular reading" because this is where you'll start your curriculum development for products.

It's a Lot Like How Writers Read

To think about how a teacher of writing would read, it might be easiest to start by thinking about how a writer would read. This is a concept many of us have used to help our students study the craft of written texts. We teach them to *read like writers*, but only after we have helped them become *like that*—like someone who writes. Like writers.

We begin by making predictable spaces and times in our classrooms where students write every single day. We encourage them to find ideas and to turn those ideas into all kinds of writing—poems, short stories, memoirs, essays. We share lots of this writing so that students grow accustomed to going public with writing. We set things up so that students write so much and so routinely that they come to see themselves as *people who write*. Out of their daily experiences, they develop a history and an identity as this kind of person and come to know themselves in this way. *I am a great poet. The best thing I've written is my article about soccer camp. Someday I'd like to write a novel. I have trouble with endings. Action is my forté.* They also come to know that, at least as long as they are with us, they are going to continue to be people who write and publish, and so they better start figuring out what they will write next.

Once our students have this identity, then we can begin to teach them to read like people who write. I often use the metaphor of a seamstress in a dress shop to explain how writers read differently than people who don't write. I tell students:

> Because my friend is a seamstress, she goes to the mall or to the dress shops differently than the rest of us who aren't seamstresses. First, it takes her a lot longer than a normal person to make her way through the store. She turns the dresses and jumpers and shirts inside out, sometimes sitting right down on the floor to study how something is made. While the rest of us mere shoppers are looking only at sizes and prices, my friend is looking closely at inseams and stitching and "cuts on the bias." She wants to know how what she sees was made, how it was put together. And the frustrating thing for anyone shopping with her is that as long as it takes her, she hardly ever buys anything! You see, my friend's not shopping for clothes, she's shopping for *ideas* for clothes. After a day at the mall she goes home

with a head full of new ideas for what she might make next on her trusty sewing machine. (Ray 1999, 13)

My friend shops differently because of who she is, a seamstress. Because sewing is something she does, she sees possibilities for her own work every time she looks closely at the work of other seamstresses. This is the way a writer reads. Writers can't help but notice how things are written as they read because every encounter with a written text is an opportunity to learn their craft.

Frank Smith says that when writers read they are always learning how written language works, how it goes. "The learning," Smith says, "is unconscious, effortless, incidental, vicarious, and essentially collaborative" (Smith 1988, 21). And just look at what writers say in response to the question, "What advice would you give someone who wants to write?" I have dozens and dozens of quotes from different writers responding to this question and they almost all say some version of, "Read. You need to read widely if you want to be a writer."

The jump, then, is not a long one. We know that we must also read widely if we are to be teachers of writing. And we can't just read, we have to read like the people we are. We have to read with a sense of the future, knowing that any time we're reading stories or editorials or poems, it is just a matter of time before we'll be teaching our students how to write stories and editorials and poems.

Text as Curriculum Potential: What Can We Learn from Single Texts

Every act of reading, then, can essentially be an act of curriculum development for us as teachers of writing. Every single text we encounter represents a whole chunk of curriculum, a whole set of things to know about writing. Every single text has a beginning, middle, and end, and some way to get from one to the other. Every single text has words formed into sentences, and many have sentences chunked into paragraphs. All texts are demonstrations of some writer's decisions about word choice, voice, perspective. All texts are demonstrations of some genre potential. All texts are demonstrations of how our language works and its conventions. Most all texts have punctuation and capitalization . . . every single text is a whole chunk of curriculum potential.

As teachers of writing, over time we develop a sort of general habit of mind that always asks of the well-written texts we encounter, "Okay, now how's this written?" Sometimes we ask this question very deliberately as we are reading purposefully as teachers of writing, studying the kinds of texts we are going to teach our students how to write. And sometimes the question just occurs to us when we're reading for other reasons—as I was at breakfast that morning. We think to ourselves in the midst of that reading, *Hmm . . . look at how that's written.* This habit of mind leads us to all we need to know about how our written language works and how a writer makes it work well.

With the curriculum of process, we want to know what kinds of things writers think about and what kinds of things they do as they find ideas, grow those ideas into drafts, and then revise and edit those drafts for publication. In contrast, with the curriculum of products, we need specific knowledge about how all kinds of written texts *work*. We are always using that general question, "How's this written?" to develop this curriculum knowledge, but we find that as we ask that question we are led again and again to look at particular aspects of the workings of texts.

> ### Thinking It Through...
>
> Before reading the questions that follow, you might want to get a familiar text (any kind of writing) in your hands. It should be one you know well and think is a smashing example of good writing. As you read on, look between your text and these questions and see what curriculum your text has to offer.

For example, imagine having a single, well-written text in our hands. We can look very specifically at that text and find out all kinds of things about writing. We can ask questions of that text like these:

General Approach to the Writing
◆ What's the piece about? How does this help us think about topic selection?

- What is the approach to the writing? Is there more than one form operating in the piece?
- What do we think the author was intending to do with this piece of writing? Tell a story? Describe? Celebrate? Share a memory? Make a point? Compare two things? Help us see something in a new way? Provide information? Etc., etc., etc. . . . How does this help us think about the work different forms of writing can do?
- How is the piece focused? What's included, and what do you think has been left out?
- Who is narrating the piece?
- What genre-specific things can you learn from looking at this piece? For example, what does it teach you about character development in a piece of fiction or placement of your argument in an editorial, etc.?

Construction of the Text
- How does the title relate to the text?
- How does it start?
- How does it end?
- Looking at the text as a whole, what different parts do we see? How do the parts of it work together? How does the text *move*?
- Are there parts embedded within parts—dialogue, side stories, explanations, etc.

Making the Language Work
- What interesting work are the various parts of speech doing in the text: verbs, nouns, pronouns, adjectives, adverbs, conjunctions, interjections, prepositions?
- What is the writer doing with sentences in the text?
- What interesting punctuation choices has the writer made in this

text? How is the punctuation supporting the meaning and the sound of the text?

◆ If the text is divided into paragraphs, what paragraph work do you see the writer doing?

◆ Does the writer manipulate any conventions to make meanings?

◆ Is print used in any interesting ways to convey meaning?

◆ Which parts of the text have really nice *sound*? What's the writer doing in these places?

Questions of Picture Books Specifically

◆ What is the overall approach to the illustrations?

◆ How are the illustrations used to make meaning in the text?

◆ What work do the illustrations do independently of the written text?

◆ Where are the words in relation to the illustrations?

◆ Do the illustrations seem to operate in any structured way? Do they work together a certain way?

◆ What are the focal points of the illustrations and how do they relate to the text? What decisions has the illustrator made about focus?

Most texts give us at least one answer to all these questions, and every one of those answers is something we can know about writing—its curriculum. For a beginning example (we'll look at lots more in later chapters), let's say we are studying Bob Graham's book *"Let's Get a Pup!" Said Kate* (2001) and we think there's this one part where the writing has a really neat sound to it. It comes right after the family in the book sees Dave, the puppy they will eventually take home from the pound. The part we like goes like this and is spaced on the page like this:

> He was small.
> He was cute.
> He was brand-new.

When we think about what the writer is doing, we realize he has chosen not to use his sentence-combining skills for these three details and has instead written three short sentences in a row and constructed them exactly the same way. We also notice that the adjectives have about the same number of syllables—one, one, and two. The sentences have a nice rhythm to them, and now we know one specific way to make writing have nice rhythm: *you can write a series of short sentences using the same sentence construction for each, and using words with about the same number of syllables.*

When we study texts with questions like these in mind, every answer is curriculum, and this is why a single well-written text is so full of potential. Now the trick, of course, is to remember that while most any text can give us answers to all these questions, it is only *one* text. If we stack five texts up, say five feature articles, we might very well find five different answers to, "How does it start?" and five different answers to, "What was the author intending to do in the piece?" and five different answers to most of the questions we ask of the texts. Over time we will want to read widely so that we can show our students a good range of options for how to make all kinds of different texts work.

Thinking It Through...

If you're reading in a study group and everyone looked at different texts with these questions in mind, you might spend some time talking about what you found. Look for connections and disconnections. Try naming some of your insights as general curriculum statements.

Sometimes we will want to take questions like those I have listed and research them very specifically in texts we admire to generate curriculum for a specific unit of study. Often we invite our students to do this with us in a mini-inquiry around some specific writing question. But much of our best curriculum will come to us when we least expect it. We'll be just reading along, by the pool or in bed at night, and all of a sudden we'll think, *Why, would you look at that. How cool . . . I'll have to show this to my students.* The things we notice like this, the striking features of well-written texts, will certainly help us answer these questions, but in our day-to-day reading we simply let the texts show us what they have to offer. We learn to trust that, with experience, our eyes will begin to see possibilities everywhere.

References

Graham, Bob. 2001. *"Let's Get a Pup!" Said Kate.* Cambridge, MA: Candlewick Press.

Pitts, Leonard. (Oct. 7, 1999). "Offended by the News Media? We're So Sorry." *Asheville Citizens Times.* A7.

Ray, Katie Wood. 1999. *Wondrous Words: Writers and Writing in the Elementary Classroom.* Urbana, IL: NCTE.

Smith, Frank. 1988. *Joining the Literacy Club: Further Essays into Education.* Portsmouth, NH: Heinemann.

CHAPTER 7

From Reading to Writing Curriculum

As teachers of writing, the key to curriculum development for the products of writing is to learn to read differently. We read for meaning, as we have all our lives, but we also read to see *how* things are written. Seeing this helps us know what to teach our students about how to write things. All the curriculum knowledge we need for products is waiting for us on our bookshelves and in our magazine racks and tucked in our newspaper stands out by the road. Professional authors are just waiting to co-teach with us and show our students (and us) how to write well.

To read like teachers of writing, we use a predictable, recursive line of thinking that is very similar to the one we used to find process curriculum in our writing experiences. You may remember that in Chapter Two we looked at these two similar lines of thinking side by side. We'll do that again here.

You may be curious about that word *craft*. The craft of the writing is the final *product*ion of it, the way that it is fashioned in a finished form for publication. In essence, developing the curriculum of products is developing a knowledge base of crafting techniques (moves) writers use to write well. When we notice writers writing well in the texts we read, we use this recursive line of thinking to look closely at that writing, figure out exactly what moves the writer is making,

Craft Study Thinking	Process Study Thinking
NOTICE something in the text.	NOTICE (or look at) something you have done or thought about as a writer.
TALK ABOUT IT and MAKE A THEORY about why the writer might have crafted it this way.	DESCRIBE what you have done or thought about, and why you did it or thought about it.
NAME what it is, exactly, the writer is doing in the text.	NAME, in some generalized way, what you did or thought about.
CONNECT IT, if you can, to another text you know in which a writer is doing the same thing.	CONNECT what you have done or thought about, if you can, to another writer's process.
ENVISION yourself or your students making this same craft move in your writing.	ENVISION your students doing this or thinking this as they write.

and then envision how it would go if we or our students made those same moves in our own writing. When we get all the way to envisioning crafting moves from the writing we see, we have moved to a specific act of curriculum development. We have developed an understanding of something we can show students how to do.

Let's work through an example of this reading like a teacher of writing in action, and as we do, keep in mind that this is a familiar line of thinking that begins with noticing and ends with a new vision of something that's possible in writing.

Reading Like a Teacher in Action

Notice

Gary Smith is one of my favorite co-teachers of writing. He writes mostly feature articles for *Sports Illustrated*. His writing is always well crafted, and my visions of what's possible in writing get broader every time I read his work. I recently purchased a collection of his sports writing entitled *Beyond the Game* and was reading it while waiting in the doctor's office. About halfway through an article about Magic Johnson's return to the NBA from retirement (Smith 2000, 99–115), I caught myself noticing something very interesting in the writing.

The "big idea" of the whole piece was that there were so many signs that Magic Johnson was wanting to return to the NBA, the writer couldn't believe he hadn't predicted it, hadn't seen it coming before the actual announcement was made. The very interesting thing I noticed was that, though he obviously seemed to be referring to himself in the piece, Smith kept using a second-person "you," instead of the first-person pronoun "I." He started it right in the beginning of the piece like this:

> When the sunlight and the angle are right, you can see your face on the screen of your computer. Staring back at you through the words of the story you've already halfway written on Ervin (Magic) Johnson's contented life in retirement. How could this have happened to you?
>
> You *believed* him. You, who surely should have learned your lesson a dozen years ago, listening to a fat, happy minister named George Foreman swear to you he could never close his hands into fists and strike a man again.
>
> You, who wrote about the whiplash Muhammad Ali and Sugar Ray Leonard felt each time they tried to retire from the sport at which they were geniuses. (99)

I saw the "you" being used here in the lead to the article, but it was really halfway through when I realized he was writing the whole piece referring to himself with the "you" pronoun. Between each vignette about Magic Johnson, Smith embeds commentary about how he should have seen the signs coming, each time referring to himself, Smith, as "you." Just a couple of examples:

> Everything you needed to know about Ervin and the NBA, you had time to figure out in that pause. (107)

Perhaps it was his charisma that disarmed you. Beheaded you. Gelded you. (109)

And finally, in the closing sentences of the article:

And you know what? You believe him. Absolutely. (115)

So this is what I noticed Gary Smith doing that made me stop, reread, and begin to think like a teacher of writing.

Talk about it, make a theory

Because I was alone in a place crowded with strangers when I noticed this writing move, I actually *thought* about it, instead of talked about it. I wondered why Smith would choose to write the piece this way. It is so clear that he is talking about himself, about how *he* missed all these signs that Magic would return to the NBA. Why not just write it in first person?

I reread and thought some more. The "you" voice engaged me in the piece in a very direct way. As I read, I found myself thinking, along with Gary Smith, *Can't you see hints in what Magic is doing? In what he's saying?* I found myself wondering, *Would* you, Katie, *have predicted this superstar's return if you had access to all this inside information that Smith had?*

> **Thinking It Through…**
>
> *You might want to get another familiar text (different from the one you looked at in the last chapter) and work your way through this line of thinking with me. Begin by just reading and seeing what strikes you first about how it's written. It can be anything, but make sure you can point to it specifically in the text.*

I realized that by writing about himself as "you," Gary Smith succeeded in generalizing his experience, in transposing it upon me as his reader. He created some distance with the "you"—just enough distance to make me feel *his* story could actually be *my* story. I could hear echoes from many years past when I used a similar technique in pleading various cases with my mom. "But mom, when *you're* out having fun with everybody and *you're* talking and stuff, *you're* not

Thinking It Through… ↺

If you're walking through this process with your own text, stop now and show someone what you noticed. Talk about it and help that person see what you see in the writing.

thinking about what time it is!" I was really talking about myself, of course, but somehow the "you" made it about more than me. The "you" was an attempt to make my case "every man's" case, and hopefully my mom's case as well so she would understand better. (For the record, it usually didn't work.)

I thought about the many texts I know where a second-person "you" was used to make the reader feel as if he or she were some other creature—texts like Joanne Ryder's *Shark in the Sea* (1997): "You are a great white shark, a fish, a giant, ever moving day and night, breathing below the surface, hunting slyly out of sight." But this isn't what Gary Smith is doing. It is so clear that the "you" in the piece is really him, really the one narrating it for us.

Naming

I tried to name, as specifically as I could, what I thought it was Gary Smith was doing. Basically, the naming I did went like this: Gary Smith wrote from some-

Thinking It Through… ↺

With your own text, try to name as specifically as you can what it is the writer is doing. Spell it out. You may need to use grammatical vocabulary to do it, but don't shy away from that. This is where our knowledge of how the language works really matters. Go ahead and think about what you might call this writing move you've noticed—if it doesn't already have a name.

thing that is clearly a first-person experience, but chose to write it in second person, referring to himself as "you" instead of "I," so that the experience becomes one the reader can feel for herself, can feel like the "you" to whom all this is happening. Gary Smith pulled off an eloquent, "you for I switch" in his writing. This is how I will think of it in my mind—a "you for I switch."

This naming exactly what the writer is doing is important at two levels for me as I read like a teacher of writing. On one level, having named it in this way will help me recognize it when I see it again in my reading. I know that my understanding of how writers do this particular thing will grow even deeper as I encounter more and more examples of it across texts. And on another level, naming it, saying what the writer has done in very explicit terms, will help me try and do it myself. By naming what Gary Smith did, I have essentially written myself instructions for doing the same thing. And if I can envision doing it, then I can teach someone else how to do it.

Connect it

Now, it is important to note that when I noticed Gary Smith doing this "you for I switch" in his piece this particular morning, it may not have been the first time I have read something written like this. Actually, I would imagine I have read things written like this many times in my years and years of reading. I may have even written something like this myself. But this was the first time I had really noticed it at a conscious level. This was the first time I had ever stopped, reread it, and tried to figure out exactly what the writer was doing. This was the first time I had read something like this *like a teacher of writing,* and reading it in this way gave me new eyes to recognize it when I came across it again. It didn't take long.

A few days later, browsing through books at a conference, I picked up a picture book, *Cecil's Story* (1991), written by George Ella Lyon. Just two or three pages into the book I realized I had come upon another writer doing the same thing Gary Smith had done. The first sentence, running across two page spreads, reads like this: "If your papa went off to war, he might get hurt and your mama might go to fetch him." In the first spread, Peter Catalanotto's beautiful watercolor paintings show a young boy sitting with his mother at the dinner table, the father clearly absent. In the second spread, the boy and his dog stand at a fence and look longingly out across fields and into a sunset. As the sad but hopeful piece continues, it becomes increasingly clear that the young boy reappearing in each picture is actually the boy to whom all this is happening. The boy whose father has gone away to war. The boy who is Cecil, the narrator.

Thinking It Through...

Go ahead and try and think of another example of a text where a writer is doing the same thing you've noticed. Don't be alarmed if you can't think of one right away. You might talk with others and see if they can think of a connecting text example from their reading experiences.

With words and pictures, George Ella Lyon and Peter Catalalotto, in a *very* different kind of text, made the same crafting decision that Gary Smith made. The pictures let us know that we clearly have a first-person narrator, though the entire piece is actually written as it is in the opening line, with a second-person "you." My understanding of how this crafting technique works grew deeper as I studied it in yet another, very different text.

Often, some time passes before I am reading and I realize a writer is making some crafting move I have noticed and thought about before. But I always trust that this *will* happen because I have come to realize that the techniques writers use to craft their writing, the things they know how to do with words and sentences and the shapes of whole texts, these things are more alike than different. There are very distinct ways written texts can work, and reading in this way helps me uncover them and come to own them as a teacher and a writer.

Envision

Noticing what Gary Smith was doing in this article and thinking about it in this way leaves me with a very clear vision of something that is possible in writing, something specific a writer can decide to do, something specific I can now teach. At the end of this line of thinking I am left with a general curriculum statement: *when narrating a piece that is clearly a first-person experience, you might choose to write it in second person with the pronoun "you" instead of in first person with "I." This helps generalize your experience for your reader and make it seem like it's more his or her experience.*

To turn this thing I know about writing into powerful curriculum, I have to be able to envision a writer deciding to write a piece in this way. I think of a scenario. Perhaps it's a piece about something very sad, the death of a beloved pet, for instance. I can envision a writer using this "you for I switch" and the piece going something like this:

> You know that it will happen someday. You know your dog will not always be with you. You know it in your head, but your heart is just never ready when it happens. . . .

It's important to carry my thinking far enough that I actually envision a topic and some beginning text that would go like this. I have to be able to actually write something using this technique if I am really to own it as curriculum knowledge and be able to present it as an option a writer might try.

Thinking It Through…

First, write a general curriculum statement for the technique (or move) you have noticed. Next (the hard part), try and write something and use language or text as you've stated it can be used in your general statement. Make sure you use a totally different topic and different words—though you may need to use the same kinds of words (parts of speech).

Examining Core Beliefs

So there it is, a line of thinking so similar to the one we used to develop curriculum for the process of writing, ending in that same important place, "What can this help my students understand or be able to do on their own as writers?" We always push curriculum development until it ends with that vision, looking at each thing we notice in a text until we get to that point: something we can now teach a writer how to do. And just like the stories of our own writing experiences are rich with curriculum, any single well-written text is full of things to know about writing too.

If we use this line of thinking to move from reading to writing curriculum, we do it with some core beliefs about curriculum development guiding us. We need to be articulate about what these beliefs are so they are open for our reflection when we run into bumps and hard parts along the way. Let's think those beliefs through a little here now.

Match reading to writing

First, we believe that the best way to learn to write anything is to read the kind of thing you are learning to write. To write poetry, read poetry. To write feature articles, read feature articles. To write memoir, read memoir. Writers must first be readers. And of course it follows that to *teach* anyone how to write anything we must first be readers of that kind of writing as well. The curriculum of poetry is found in poetry, the curriculum of feature articles is found in feature articles, of memoir, in memoir.

Thinking It Through...

Think about what kinds of writing you need to add to your collection for your teaching. Off the top of your head, do you know good examples of the different kinds of writing you will be asking students to try in the writing workshop? If not, think about where you'll need to look to find good examples of this kind of writing.

The first curricular move we make, then, is to ask this question, "What are all the different kinds of things students might write for publication?" We collect these things and we especially go in search of the kinds of things that are like what our students might write. We fill our writing workshops up with examples of all kinds of writing, all kinds of things students might write. We know that our students will need to read the kinds of things they're going to write, and we know as teachers we'll generate our curriculum from reading in this way too.

Understanding language use

Next, we believe that everything we need to know about how our written language works is found in actual written texts. We believe that good authors are people who know a lot about how our language works and who know how to use it well for all kinds of purposes. And for this reason, we believe good authors make the best teachers of writing.

We understand that grammar books and usage manuals are meant to describe language as it is generally used (its conventions), but that they did not exist *before* the language itself. In this sense, these books don't set how the language is used. The language sets what goes in these books.

We believe language use is a uniquely human endeavor and is full of wondrous potential, and that writers need to know *so much* about it so they can use it to its fullest potential. And we believe that to really understand language with this depth, writers have to look closely at how it is actually used in well-written texts. All our curriculum about how the language works, then, comes from looking at it when it's used *well*. We always back up this curriculum with examples from these texts.

Thinking It Through… ↻

Remember that the minute we say, "You can't do that" in writing, we'll often find a writer who's found an interesting way to do just that—whatever the "that" may be. You might want to go search and collect some text examples where writers are doing things you thought they weren't supposed to do. See if you can figure out why writers are deciding to make language work in these ways.

We believe that students need to be able to speak the *language* of language if they are to be writers. So as we look closely at well-written texts with them, we use parts of speech names and literary and usage terms to help them name what they are noticing in these texts. We do not study these *separately* from the study of good writing, however. We simply embed these terms in all our conversations about what students see in texts and what we show them in texts—even in kindergarten. If a five-year-old says, "I love how it says 'the snake slithered,'" then we say back to him, "Yes, isn't that an amazing verb—*slithered*." Over time in school, speaking the language of language can become second nature to children if they are used to hearing it spoken in natural contexts.

Writing is individual, but not unique

We believe that writing technique or style is more alike than it is different, that it is individual in its use, but not unique. Written language, by its very definition, is something we *share*. It couldn't be language, a tool for communication, if we didn't use it in very similar ways that others recognize and understand. We know that two different writers can employ the exact same way of using language in very different kinds of texts—a feature article published in an adult magazine (Gary Smith, *Sports Illustrated*) and a picture book of historical fiction (George Ella Lyon, *Cecil's Story*), as we've seen in the previous example.

We take this knowledge and realize we can generate curriculum from almost any kind of writing, about almost any topic. We also know that as we develop the curriculum of products, over time we want to develop collections of examples of different writers doing the exact same things with language in very different kinds of texts. These collections help our students understand ways of shaping texts and using language across many different topics, writing in many different forms and genres, and for many different purposes and audiences.

References

Lyon, George Ella. 1991. *Cecil's Story*. Illustrated by Peter Catalanotto. New York: Orchard Books.

Ryder, Joanne. 1997. *Shark in the Sea*. Illustrated by Michael Rothman. New York: Morrow Junior Books.

Smith, Gary. 2000. "True Lies." In *Beyond the Game: The Collected Sportswriting of Gary Smith*, 99–115. New York: Atlantic Monthly Press.

CHAPTER 8

Getting Started Developing the Curriculum of Products

W hen we first start trying to teach ourselves to read like teachers of writing, we often struggle because we've never really looked at texts this way. We pick a book or a magazine article up and we think, *Okay, I'm looking at it, but I'm not noticing anything.* And we panic because, even if we understand the whole line of thinking, we know we can't go anywhere until we notice something. We have to move forward and trust that once we train our eyes to look at how texts are written (in addition to what they're about), it will get easier and easier, and before long it will start to snowball. We'll know more about how to write well than we'll even need.

One thing that helps us find our footing and get started is to see a fair number of examples of the kinds of things other people notice in texts—people who've had a lot of experience reading in this way. That's what we'll do in this chapter. We'll look at just a selected few examples of the kinds of things we might notice in texts and collect for our teaching. We'll let these examples demonstrate how a teacher of writing might read differently, and then later in the appendices we'll list resources of texts and text examples like these that we might use in our teaching.

Before we look at examples though, one point seems worth making. As teachers of writing, we can find examples of good writing *anywhere*. Knowing this, we do two things. First, we carry on with our reading lives—the ones we'd have even if we weren't teachers of writing—knowing that we'll routinely see things we might cut out or copy for our teaching. We're not purposeful as teachers in this reading, we just know it happens—every now and then we'll come across great stuff. Second, we read *on purpose* for our teaching. We read texts that are like the kinds we'll be teaching our students to write—in genre, form, length, style, and audience. These may or may not be things we would read on our own, but for our teaching we must read and study these texts to develop our curriculum knowledge.

So what kinds of things do we notice as we read like teachers of writing? Basically, we notice the kinds of things we know someone facing a draft needs to know. There are lots of these things, but to simply demonstrate the kinds of things we notice, we will lump them into the four broad categories here:

◆ General approach to the writing
◆ Construction of the text
◆ Making the language work
◆ Making pictures work with texts (for our youngest writers and for those writing for young audiences)

As teachers of writing, we have to take what we notice and think about it until we can name the specific curriculum in what we see. Then we make certain we can envision it as a possibility for our students' writing. We have to have a sort of spirit of adventure and an active imagination to think things through that far—all the way to envisioning it as a possibility. But we'll demonstrate that as we go along.

General Approach to the Writing

You may remember that in Chapter Four we said that the move from a notebook or an idea to a draft is essentially a move to begin *making* something. What kinds of things can writers make? The answer to this question can be as big as topic and genre, but it can also be much more specific than that: *I'm going to write a memoir that is a series of separate vignettes. I'm going to write an information piece, but I want it to read like a story.* This is one of the first things we're on the lookout for as teachers of writing. We look at texts just to see how they're "made." Lots of them will be texts we recognize and are very familiar—stories, poems, editorials. But when the writer has taken an interesting approach to the writing, we notice it because we know it might represent a new possibility for something one of our students could try in his or her writing.

Thinking It Through…

Think about texts you already know. How many different ways do you know that one might approach the writing of a poetry collection? A feature article? A short story? An editorial or essay? A memoir? Think of specific titles you know that represent different approaches to different types of writing.

Take two picture books by Charles R. Smith, for example. When I first saw *Rimshots: Basketball Pix, Rolls, and Rhythms* (1999), my thought was, *this is written like a collage.* There are fourteen short, separate pieces of writing in the book, and they represent all different kinds of writing. Four of them are shaped poems. One is written as a series of sentences that begin with "I remember . . ." One is just a whole bunch of quotations entitled "Excuses," and they're all things people say as excuses when they're not playing well. One is written in present tense, first person and it follows the in-the-moment action of playing one-on-one. Two are written in straight prose and are memoir-y accounts of players. One is a page of quotations of inspiration, one is an internal monologue of a player who wants to go in the game, one a dialogue between a young player and an older player, and so on.

Rimshots is a really cool way to write about a topic and it gives us visions for a kind of writing our students might try. A student writing about his experiences at summer camp, for example, might write it as a collage of different kinds of writing like this. Or even a high school student writing a college application essay might choose to craft it as a collage much like Smith's basketball piece. *You can write about a topic as a collage of different kinds of writing.*

In the picture book *Loki & Alex* (2001), Smith shows us another interesting approach to the writing. Loki is a dog and Alex is his owner. The book is written in first person and it alternates back and forth, first Alex narrating and then Loki, as the two share with us their different takes on their life together. The curriculum vision this gives us: *you can move alternately between two narrators in your text*—is an interesting way to compare and contrast two views on a topic. We can imagine a student writing about, say, a new baby in the family might set the text up this way. The writer could look at things like feeding time and waking up in the night and getting dressed from the baby's perspective and then from the mom or a sibling's perspective. Or a college student writing an essay about what it's like to live in a different culture might look at *Loki & Alex* and get an idea to shift the sections back and forth between his life and a person's life in a different culture.

Sometimes we notice writing because there seems to be more than one form operating in the piece. Take Karen Hesse's two works of historical fiction, for example. *Out of the Dust* (1997) and *Witness* (2001) both say "a novel" on their covers. And yet, when you look inside, you see that the form is actually narrative poetry. *Out of the Dust* is a series of narrative poems that move through time to tell the story (each poem is dated), and *Witness* is a series of narrative poems that move through time and voice. Eleven different "characters" take turns narrating the poems that tell the story, and the sections are labeled as "acts" lending the quality of a drama to the collection as well.

Knowing these two books we know that *one way to write a story (it wouldn't have to be historical fiction) is to write it as a series of narrative poems.* And we even have more than one vision for how to organize these poems as text and move the narrative along: *you can move them through time with a single narrator; or you can move them through time with different narrators.* Any one of our students who has a story to tell—about a soccer tournament or a fishing trip or anything— could try writing it in this way. And of course, a student could write any kind of fiction (historical, realistic, science, etc.) and approach the writing in this way.

Sometimes we notice very simple things that actually frame the whole approach to the writing. Joy Cowley's *Red-Eyed Tree Frog* (1999), for example, is written in straight present tense, as if the action is happening right as you read it: "The tree frog is no longer hungry. It climbs onto a leaf." A simple thing, but it represents such possibility: *you can write it like it's happening right now.* We can just imagine one of our youngest students writing in this way about, say, riding his bike: "I pedal as hard as I can. I climb the hill . . ." And even our more sophisticated writers might get a vision for writing scenes in longer texts in straight present tense.

Thinking It Through...

At this point, you might want to stop and think about the texts you know. Can you think of others where the approach to the writing is the same as the ones we've described so far? Many texts use the same approach to the writing, and over time we want to create short stacks of these texts for our teaching.

Often, we notice the approach to writing in the feature articles, editorials, and essays we read. In Rick Reilly's back-page piece "Going for the Jugular" in the May 29, 2000, issue of *Sports Illustrated* (86), he writes what is clearly an opinion piece about former Indiana basketball coach Bobby Knight. But instead of stating his opinion and then elaborating three supporting reasons (by the way, I've never seen him write an opinion piece that way), Reilly writes the piece as if we are listening in on an interview with Knight. As he sets the story of the fictional interview up, he tells us, "The questions will come from the *Terre Haute Banner's* backup sidebar writer, 19-year-old Tiffany Jo Flowers." As the interview proceeds and we see how the coach responds to Tiffany Jo, Knight's character is revealed (according to Reilly, of course). We get a pretty clear picture of Reilly's opinion of the coach and his predicament.

Noticing this, we now know, *one way to reveal a person's character is to create a fictional scene where we get to see how that person responds and interacts with others.* Reilly chose to create the scene of an interview with a reporter, but it wouldn't have to be an interview. It could have been Knight walking into a diner or Knight driving in the car with his wife—any scene that would reveal character. We also know that, *one way to express an opinion is to create a fictional scene that clearly reveals how you see an issue.* We can imagine that a writer we teach might use this same approach to write an opinion piece. Perhaps the writer might create a scene that reveals his or her opinion of a controversial celebrity or historical figure—Madonna at a PTO meeting or Napoleon eating breakfast with his troops.

We'll move on now, but hopefully that gives us a picture of the kinds of things we notice when we are looking at general ways to approach the writing. In Appendix A, you will find a selected resource list of all types of texts that help us envision new possibilities for ways we and our students might approach writing.

Construction of the Text

At some point in the drafting process, the writer has to figure out how to make all the parts—from start to finish—work together. Sometimes writers have a really good picture of how this is going to happen before they ever start drafting, and sometimes they have done a good bit of drafting before they start to see how the pieces will take shape. But either way, writers need visions for how to get texts started, move them along, and end them with a sigh, a bang, or whatever feeling they want the reader to have. So one of the things we notice is how the actual parts of the text work together. Sometimes we call this particular aspect *structure*.

We might notice, for example, that Cynthia Rylant's picture book *In November* (2000) and Eileen Spinelli's picture book *In My New Yellow Shirt*

(2001) are both really written as lists—one a list of descriptions and images of November, and one a list of things a little boy can imagine himself being in his new yellow shirt. Both authors use the title as a structural device throughout the text, repeating it to begin each new section of text.

This type of repetition is a very common way of making text work together, and it is used across all kinds of writing with all kinds of topics. Rick Reilly used it so elegantly in his back-page piece on Oct. 1, 2001 in *Sport Illustrated*, "It's a Whole New Ball Game." He writes a long list of things he hopes for the world in the aftermath of the September 11, 2001 terrorists attacks, beginning each one with the repeating phrase, "Let's hope." Here's one of my favorites:

> Let's hope the terrorists' attacks will put an end to the look-at-me chest thumps after a two yard gain. Pal, unless you went up a flaming skyscraper when everyone else was coming down, we don't want to hear about it. (88)

And of course, Dr. Martin Luther King, Jr. used the same structure to fashion just a section of text, "I have a dream," in his famous speech for civil rights.

When we notice this in texts, we know, *one way to write a text is as a list* and we also know *one way to mark the move from one item on the list to the next is to use a repeating phrase.* We can imagine students using this same text structure to write about all kinds of things. A descriptive piece about camping, for example, might work something like this:

> When you're camping in the mountains, the air is clear and fresh. The trees move slightly in the breeze, and the water rushes over rocks nearby. Every sound is part of the music of mountains, and your heart sings along.
>
> When you're camping in the mountains, you feel a thousand miles away from everything, even though you aren't . . .

In Eileen Spinelli's picture book *Summerbath, Winterbath* (2001), we notice that the text really has two sides to it. It's a descriptive piece set in the early 1900s that compares taking baths in an old metal washtub in summer and then in winter. Spinelli writes all about summer baths first, and then switches and writes all about winter baths. This is in contrast to alternating between two things you are comparing, which is how Cynthia Rylant shows us the two sides of a scarecrow's life in her picture book *Scarecrow* (1998). To show contrast, Rylant's text moves back and forth between descriptive passages about the scarecrow's shabby, thrown-together outward appearance and the miraculous world of growing things all around him to which he bears witness day after day.

Looking closely at these two texts, we see the two most common structures for comparing and contrasting: *you can describe everything about one side of your comparison, then switch and show everything about the other side,* that's one way, or *you can alternate between the two as the text moves along.* Any one of our students writing about a topic that lends itself to comparison and contrast could use these texts to get a vision for how to make those texts work— a piece comparing two grandparents or two siblings, a piece comparing night to day or one kind of music to another or two sports, a piece comparing how things used to be to how they are now, for whatever reason.

We might notice in Trish Cooke's picture book *The Grandad Tree* (2000) how she moves the middle section along by showing a single detail, the tree, across the four seasons of the year. It's a beautiful piece about a grandfather who has passed away and the tree is an anchor image in the text. Right in the middle of the text, four consecutive sentences describe the tree in each season. It's a very focused way to show the passage of time: *you can take a single detail and move it across markers of time, seasons, months, years (it doesn't have to be seasons).* Pam Muñoz Ryan uses days of the week as markers to move through time in her picture book *Mice and Beans* (2001), but instead of focusing it with just one detail, she actually moves the events of the story through the days. This gives us another vision: *you can move the events of a narrative through markers of time, days of the week, hours of the day, months, etc.*

Our students could use these structural devices across so many kinds of writing. The student writing about the home run he hit in the ninth inning of the baseball game might use Cooke's method of getting us through lots of innings fast. He could take the single detail of say, his heart racing, and run it through several innings to get us to the ninth:

> In the first inning it was just a little thump in my chest. By the third inning it was beginning to gallop, and by the seventh it was a full fledged roar. When my time to bat came in the ninth, I thought my heart would explode right there on the mound.

Something like that. We use what we notice about how texts are constructed to help our students envision new possibilities for structuring their own texts. In Appendix B, you'll find a selected resource list of other texts that show students strong text structures they can try in their own writing.

Thinking It Through... ⟲

You might try envisioning other texts using the different structures we've looked at in this section. Remember, we don't really own curriculum knowledge until we can envision how it would be used to write another text.

Making the Language Work

There are lots and lots of things to notice about how the language actually works to build strong stories, poems, and editorials. Here we are noticing interesting word choices, uses of punctuation, construction of sentences and paragraphs, and here we have to really think about how we'd make language work like this in another text. We actually have to compose a little to envision.

Sometimes a single passage can hold a whole "chunk" of curriculum potential. Let's take, for example, this passage from Mary Lyn Ray's picture book *Pumpkins* (1992).

> All over the world—in Kiev, Killarney, Khartoum and Tashkent, in Quito, Quebec, Cairo and Cadiz—there were jack-o'-lanterns being carved. There were pumpkin pies baking and muffins muffining.

If we look closely at this passage, there are several things to learn about how to make the language work well. Let's just list them as curriculum, knowing that any one of these could be the whole basis for a minilesson or a conference with a student. With each curriculum piece, we'll write another example just to untie it from Mary Lyn Ray's text.

◆ *You can use proper nouns to make a general noun more specific.*
◆ *One way to set a list off is with dashes.*
  "Riders of all kinds of motorcycles—Hondas, Ducatis, BMWs, Suzukis, Yamahas, Harleys—came together to ride for a good cause."
◆ *When writing a list of things, try matching initial sounds in words.*
  "We ate peanuts and pecans, truffles and tripe, bric and bread and brownies."
◆ *When writing a list of things, you might join them in different ways.*
  "I met so many interesting people—fireman, doctors, lawyers and teachers, students, waiters, salesmen and preachers."
◆ *You can use a noun as a verb, even if it is not typically used as a verb.*
  "The spot of oil on the driveway rainbowed in the morning sun after the rain."

Rich little passages, and especially richer, longer texts are just full of things to know about how the language can work, if we look at them closely. Sometimes we notice a writer take a risk to use language in a really interesting way. Take the 671-word sentence that Rick Reilly (you've probably figured out—Reilly co-teaches with me a lot) wrote in his *Sports Illustrated* back-page piece of January 10, 2000, "What's Not to Like?" The piece begins with Reilly's son asking him who he's "dissin'" this week. Reilly is shocked that his son would see it this way because, as he goes on to so elaborately explain, he loves sports. He begins the 671-word sentence with the simple phrase, "I told him I love . . ."

and then the other 666 words make up a list of all the things he loves, all of them joined by the conjunction *and* rather than with commas:

> I love the penalty box and starting blocks and "Rock, chalk, Jayhawk!" and NFL Films spirals and eye black and ear holes and slobbermouth tackles and multimillionaires piling on each other with glee and . . . (84)

It's an amazing sentence, written on purpose by a crafty writer. When we see it, we know—*sometimes you can write an amazingly long, runaway sentence as a way of overstating your case.* Now, I'll save us all the burden of actually writing a sentence like that as an example, but let's imagine a student using this technique. Let's say a student was writing an opinion piece about parents thinking teenagers have it too easy today, that they have nothing really to worry about. The piece could open with setting that idea up, and then have a runaway sentence beginning with, "We have to worry about . . ." The sentence would be completed with a very long list of all the worries teenagers do have. It's an interesting kind of risky move, but it can be very effective as it is in Reilly's piece.

Sometimes we notice a writer using a mix of sentence structure and punctuation in an interesting way, like Roger Rosenblatt in his back-page essay, "The News About Jessica," in the April 2, 2001 issue of *Time* magazine. It's a moving piece about his first grandchild and the world into which she has arrived, a world full of both bad and good. In this passage, he struggles to explain something to her, and notice how he writes it to match the struggle of speech (the ellipses are not to mark left out text—they are there as Rosenblatt uses them in the piece):

> You see, Jessica, the reason that America makes guns available to children is . . . It's this way, Jessica: some people live in slums, and others live on hills, and this is because . . . Look here, Jessica: The market goes up and the market goes down, and the explanation is . . . She is smiling now, an involuntary reflex. (84)

So we look at this passage and we know: *one way to show the struggle to find the right words is to start sentences but not finish them. Use ellipses to show them trailing off.* What's also interesting is that in this essay, this address directly to Jessica is not written as dialogue. It's simply a direct address to her in the midst of the essay—the whole piece is not addressed to her in this way—just this part. So this tells us something else: *you can directly address someone in the midst of an essay.*

We can certainly imagine a student using this technique. Let's imagine that same student writing about how parents don't understand the worries teenagers have today. Maybe that student writes a passage like this, directly addressed to her mother right in the midst of the essay:

So mom, the thing is, things get really complicated and . . . What I'm trying to say is, you've never lived like . . . Okay, this is really hard, it's just that I don't think you understand that . . . Wait, let me start over.

One thing we might notice is all the ways sentences work in texts. It is true that sentences represent complete thoughts in texts, but sometimes they are completed by the text around them. We can't really take a sentence out of a text and understand it as it is in the text. For example, sometimes sentences share a subject or a subject and a verb with another sentence. That's what Leonard Pitts is doing in this excerpt from his feature piece about seeing the movie *Saving Private Ryan:*

I've seen computer programs where war is a game and men die with synthesized squeaks. Seen movie stars with oiled biceps blow up stuntmen whose bodies turned cartwheels in the air. Seen a comedy show where Nazi soldiers were lovable boobs constantly outfoxed by their Allied captives (*Asheville Citizens Times,* Aug. 4, 1998).

Pitts uses the subject/helping verb phrase "I have" from the first sentence to serve the sentences that follow because once it's stated, it's understood. Cynthia

Rylant uses this same common construction in her picture book *Scarecrow* (1998):

> It takes a certain peace hanging around a garden all day. It takes a love of silence and air. A liking for long, slow thoughts. A friendliness towards birds.

After stating the subject and verb "It takes" in the first two sentences, she makes the phrase understood in the two sentences that follow. Looking at these two examples we know: *sometimes a series of sentences can share a subject or a subject and verb with another sentence.* It's not that they don't have them, it's just that they are understood from another sentence. So if we ask, "What's the subject and verb of the sentence 'A friendliness towards birds'?" The answer is, "It takes." We can imagine students using this technique to write something like this:

> Fear is a physically funny thing. It begins with just a feeling in your heart. A nervous gnawing deep inside you. A slight sense of things out of balance.

The second two sentences share the subject/verb "It begins" with the first sentence in the series.

So those are just a few of the kinds of things we notice when we are looking at how the language works. You'll find a list of other selected examples in Appendix C.

Making Pictures Work with Texts

Certainly for our youngest writers who compose in both pictures and text, curriculum that supports them in this composition is essential. And sometimes our more experienced writers will want to compose pieces in pictures and text as well. Books where the same person is the author and the illustrator make especially good resources for curriculum development. In these texts, we know that the composition of the pictures and the text are the result of the decision making of one person—just as the composition will be when our students write and illustrate their own texts. But we don't want to limit ourselves to just these books, as many other illustrators can show us possibilities for composing through pictures.

Thinking It Through…

This section is probably best read with a short stack of picture books in front of you. Use the discussion here as a lens to look at the books. What other things do you see happening between pictures and words in the books?

One thing we often notice as we look at these books is how the illustrations compose meaning in conjunction with the words. In Susan Rollings *New Shoes, Red Shoes* (2000), for example, the story line depends heavily on the pictures as the text is simply a labeling of what's in the pictures. But it's not a list book, it's a *story* of a little girl and her mother going shopping for new shoes the girl can wear to a party. One page, for example, says simply, "Flat shoes, summer shoes." But the picture shows a man and a woman sitting on a park bench; she's reading a book and he's eating a sandwich. From the pictures on the pages before and after we know that the mother and the daughter are passing through this park on their way to the shoe store. (By the way, per our previous discussion, the subject and verb of this sentence (and all the others in the book), are understood: <u>These people are wearing</u> flat shoes, summer shoes. This is a very common sentence construction—to have an understood subject and/or verb. You see it in all kinds of texts—not just picture books.)

This is something we see in lots of picture books—that there's more happening in the pictures than in the words—but *New Shoes, Red Shoes* is a good example of the pictures really doing the storytelling work with the words just sort of anchoring it. So we notice this and we know: *you can actually let a series of pictures tell the story and the words just label a key feature in each picture.* We can imagine a young child creating a text about, say, going fishing, and each successive picture would "tell" the story while the pages might simply read,

"Getting ready. Supplies. To the lake. Bait the hook. Wait and wait. Caught one!"

We might look at Donald Crews' *Night at the Fair* (1998) and notice that there is text actually embedded in the pictures. All kinds of "environmental print"—print that actually is in the world outside of books—is scattered throughout the text. In one spread, we see all kinds of food stands at the fair labeled with words like "Funnel Cakes" and "Cold Drinks," and on another page we see game booths with signs that read "2 In Wins." Crews has taken the print that you would naturally see at a place like this and put it right into his pictures. We notice this and we know: *you can have environmental print in your pictures in addition to the running text.* We can imagine a student creating a text about driving to her grandma's and actually putting into the pictures the names of stores and churches, the text of billboards and road signs, and other kinds of print she would pass along the way.

In Manya Stojic's book *Rain* (2000), we might notice how all the pictures of the animals waiting on the rain through the book are very close-up shots. In most of them, they are so close-up that you don't even see the whole animal. Part of each animal kind of runs off the page as she really focuses in on just the baboon's head or the rhino's snout. Even the words are written in large, bold letters as if we're seeing them close-up as well. We notice this and we know: *you can unify the pictures in your text by drawing them all with the same focus, close-up, far-away, from above or below (it wouldn't have to just be close-up).* And we can imagine a student creating a text about Christmas or a birthday and having very close-up pictures of the opened and unopened packages throughout the text, just hands of people opening them showing in the pictures.

We might notice where the pictures are in relation to the written text. For example, in Meredith Hooper's book *River Story* (2000), illustrated by Bee Willey, each two-page spread has a separated bar of space for the text. Sometimes it is on the left or right side running vertically down the spread, and sometimes the bar runs horizontally across the top or bottom of the spread.

The bar interrupts the full-page illustration, though there are tiny little illustrations inside the bar with the text. For example, the text bar on page 11 that begins, "Fed by a waterfall, bouncing down boulders" has a little circular inset picture of a fish in it. The larger illustration of the two-page spread is of a waterfall.

We notice this and we know: *you can have a separate space outside the picture for your text* and *you can put inset pictures in this space that relate to the larger picture.* The student we imagined earlier writing about driving to grandma's might actually try this and use a strip of road for the written text, separate from the illustrated scenes.

Those are just a few of the kinds of things we might notice as we study how pictures and words work together in texts. In Appendix D, you'll find a selected list of picture books and the curriculum possibilities they offer.

The best way to get started noticing is to reread the texts we know and love and ask ourselves, "What is it that the writer is doing here?" We slow our reading down and think like teachers of writing and trust good authors to show us how to write well. And in turn, we can show our students possibilities for writing well. In the next chapter, we'll look closely at the language of mini-lessons when we're teaching students the curriculum of products.

References

Cooke, Trish. 2000. *The Grandad Tree*. Illustrated by Sharon Wilson. Cambridge, MA: Candlewick Press.

Cowley, Joy. 1999. *Red-Eyed Tree Frog*. Photographs by Nic Bishop. New York: Scholastic Press.

Crews, Donald. 1998. *Night at the Fair*. New York: Greenwillow Books.

Hesse, Karen. 1997. *Out of the Dust*. New York: Scholastic Press.

————. 2001. *Witness*. New York: Scholastic Press.

Hooper, Meredith. 2000. *River Story*. Illustrated by Bee Willey. Cambridge, MA: Candlewick Press.

Pitts, Leonard. (Aug. 4, 1998). "Brutal 'Private Ryan' Crushes Misconceptions." *Asheville Citizens Times*. p. A7.

Ray, Mary Lyn. 1992. *Pumpkins*. Illustrated by Barry Root. New York: Harcourt Brace.

Reilly, Rick. (Jan. 10, 2000). "What's Not to Like?" *Sports Illustrated*. Back page.

————. (May 29, 2000). "Going for the Jugular." *Sports Illustrated*. Back page.

————. (Oct. 1, 2001). "It's a Whole New Ballgame." *Sports Illustrated*. Back page.

Rollings, Susan. 2000. *New Shoes, Red Shoes*. New York: Orchard Books.

Rosenblatt, Roger. (April 2, 2001). "The News About Jessica." *Time*. p. 84.

Ryan, Pam Muñoz. 2001. *Mice and Beans*. Illustrated by Joe Cepeda. New York: Scholastic Press.

Rylant, Cynthia. 1998. *Scarecrow*. Illustrated by Lauren Stringer. New York: Harcourt Brace.

————. 2000. *In November*. New York: Harcourt, Inc.

Smith, Charles R. 1999. *Rimshots: Basketball Pix, Rolls, and Rhythms*. New York: Dutton Children's Books.

————. 2001. *Loki & Alex: The Adventures of a Dog and His Best Friend*. New York: Dutton Children's Books.

Spinelli, Eileen. 2001. *In My New Yellow Shirt*. Illustrated by Hideko Takahashi. New York: Henry Holt.

———. 2001. *Summerbath, Winterbath*. Illustrated by Elsa Warnick. Grand Rapids, MI: Eerdman's Books for Young Readers.

Stojic, Manya. 2000. *Rain*. New York: Crown Publishers, Inc.

CHAPTER 9

Looking Closely at Minilessons
Teaching from Texts

In minilessons where we are teaching students the curriculum of products, we will be showing them possibilities for actual texts. Like minilessons of process, these minilessons have predictable rhythms and patterns to them, and they follow many of the same lines of thinking we've used throughout the book. Instead of noticing things about texts, for example, in minilessons we show students things in texts. We talk them through what we think the writer is doing. We name the technique for them in a general but explicit way, turning it into curriculum, and then we help them envision writing in this same way. Often we have crafted some text as an example of how to try what an author has shown us how to do.

When we teach minilessons like these, we teach them as part of some series of lessons within an organized unit of study. Inside a genre study of historical fiction, for example, we might teach a short series of lessons on different ways to approach the writing of this genre. Or in a study of techniques and tools for revision, we might teach a series of lessons on crafting techniques students could try in their drafts. The point is, curriculum is sturdier and carries more weight in students' work when it is organized in some way and we stay with an idea over several lessons.

We teach these kinds of minilessons as possibilities for students' work, not to give them something to do during writing time. A writing workshop begins with the understanding that students must publish a variety of pieces of writing, and then our teaching has to fill the workshop up with all kinds of ideas for what's possible in this writing. But we don't want to set agendas for our students. In other words, we don't want to teach students that one possibility for writing historical fiction is to write it as a series of narrative poems as Ann Turner does in *Mississippi Mud* (1997), and then require everyone to write a piece like this. If we do, we've taken away one of the fundamental parts of the writing process: deciding how you are going to write something. Students need to make this decision so they learn *how* to make it. We do much better teaching if, instead, we present a week's worth of minilessons on ways to approach this genre and then require students to choose one. They may choose one we have taught or one they know from their own reading, but they need to choose. Our teaching is meant to suggest many possibilities but not set courses of action for individual students.

Having said that, we may have a "try it" component to some of our minilessons, especially when we are showing students a small, contained thing such as a way to punctuate a series of sentences or a particular way to use words. We may ask them to try it quickly in their notebooks—either during the minilesson or later during their work time—but it is really more a process of trying it on "for size." They can then decide when and where and even if they need to write in this way in an actual piece they are publishing. What we want to caution ourselves against is taking over their work with our teaching agendas. Our teaching is meant to support their work, but not *become* their work.

Minilesson: Moving a Story Through Time

With all that said, let's look now at the texts of a few different minilessons. We won't need to pull out the curriculum chunks on the side as we did with lessons in process, because with the curriculum of products we are really teaching just one or two specific things from a single text example. This first lesson might be part of a series of lessons in a genre study of fiction that looks at ways to move a story through time. We begin by having students look at the opening chapter of Jerry Spinelli's *Stargirl* (2000)—the entire book is a treasure trove of curriculum on how to make the language work. It is nice when students are already familiar with a book, but if they're not that's okay too. Many of them will get interested in reading a book if you show them an excerpt of great writing. We will focus on just this part of the chapter.

From *Stargirl:*

"Did you see her?"

That was the first thing Kevin said to me on the first day of school, eleventh grade. We were waiting for the bell to ring.

"See who?" I said.

"Hah!" He craned his neck, scanning the mob. He had witnessed something remarkable; it showed on his face. He grinned, still scanning. "You'll know."

There were hundreds of us, milling about, calling names, pointing to summer-tanned faces we hadn't seen since June. Our interest in each other was never keener than during the fifteen minutes before the first bell of the first day.

I punched his arm. "Who?"

The bell rang. We poured inside.

I heard it again in homeroom, a whispered voice behind me as we said the Pledge of Allegiance:

"You see her?"

I heard it in the hallways. I heard it in English and Geometry:

"Did you see her?"

Who could it be? A new student? A spectacular blonde from California? Or from back East, where many of us came from? Or one of those summer makeovers, someone who leaves in June looking like a little girl and returns in September as a full-bodied woman, a ten-week miracle?

And then in Earth Sciences I heard a name: "Stargirl."

I turned to the senior slouching behind me. "Stargirl?" I said. "What kind of name is that?"

"That's it. Stargirl Caraway. She said it in homeroom."

"*Stargirl?*"

"Yeah."

And then I saw her. At lunch. (3–4)

Now, while there are lots of small things we might teach from this excerpt, we will focus on just three that are closely related:

- ◆ *One way to move a story through time is to have a "plot anchor" that keeps you focused and helps you leave out other details.*
- ◆ *Markers of time and place can help you move a story forward in time quickly.*
- ◆ *Shorter paragraphs can help show the reader that time is moving quickly.*

To begin the minilesson, we will read this part of the chapter with students, making sure they can see the text as we read—either from copies or from an overhead projector. Then we will launch into our teaching:

Notice...	Actual Text of Minilesson...
	When I looked at this passage, what impressed me about it was how much time passed in such a short space—the whole morning goes by in these first few short paragraphs. And then, if you just look at the rest of the chapter, we won't read it, just look, there are many more words and much longer paragraphs and only about five minutes of time pass in this longer part.
Here we're naming what it is we want them to notice in the passage.	
Demonstrating how we read like writers to figure things out.	So I studied it and I tried to put my finger on how Spinelli is moving the story through time so quickly. One thing I

Actual Text of Minilesson...

realized was that he stays focused on just one aspect of that morning—students asking "Have you seen her?" He doesn't include all kinds of details about the school or the students or other things that are happening—and you're sure lots of other things are happening. He just follows that question through the morning. This lets him move really quickly through time. It's almost like a filter—everything but that question sifts through.

I also noticed that in that sentence, "I heard it in English and Geometry: Did you see her?" He makes *two* hours pass just like that. It's like the names of the classes become time markers. And then I noticed how short the paragraphs are—especially compared to the second half of the chapter where time moves so much more slowly. You have those three in a row that are really just one or two short sentences with actions in them, "I punched . . . The bell rang . . . I heard it."

Naming the curriculum explicitly.

Showing the curriculum in use. Helps students "untie" it from the topic of the first example.

When we as teachers try writing our own examples, we are able to teach from the experience of having tried it.

So that left me with really three things I could try to make time move quickly: keep the paragraphs short with mostly just actions, find something to focus on and only look at that focus as time is passing, and use time markers like the classes. Let me show you a passage where I tried to do these three things myself:

Everything about us was tightly packed in the brand-new minivan dad had bought just for this occasion. Suitcases, bodies, nerves. Everything felt too close for comfort. And it was five o'clock in the morning.

"Buckle-up, buck-o-roos," Dad said in his way-too-cheery voice. Five reluctant clicks, and we were off.

It started, way before any of us dreamed it would.

"When are we going to get there?" my little brother whined.

We were precisely thirty-seven minutes into our family trip, driving, from South Carolina to California.

Thirty-seven minutes. I know. I looked at my watch.

"Shut up," my sister said to him. That was her official job in the family—to tell Matthew to "shut up." She took it very seriously.

Me, I turned it into a game. By estimating and averaging the approximate time between outbursts of the question, I kept myself occupied for ten states and four days.

Forty-three minutes in Alabama.

Fifteen in Texas. All the way across.

Two hours, twelve minutes in New Mexico (he took a long nap).

And by California, it was down to an average time of every five minutes, "When are we going to get there?" But by this time we were all asking it, all hungering for the ultimate prize: The Pacific Ocean.

Matthew was the first to see it. "I see it!"

"Shu," my sister began automatically.

Then she saw it too. We all saw it.

Renaming the curriculum and pointing to specific parts of the example text that illustrate it.

I tried all those things Spinelli was doing. My paragraphs are short and mostly just actions. My time markers aren't classes but states. I figured the names of states would show the family was moving along. And my focus is the little brother asking "When are we going to get there?" That way I left out all the other details of a trip that went on for days and got the reader from South Carolina to California is just a small space of text.

Helping them envision trying this and naming the curriculum once again.

So this is something that might help you as you're drafting your stories and need to move through time quickly. At some point, you might try this. Keep the paragraphs short and focused on actions, find a focus, and use time markers. Like let's see . . . let's just make something up. If you were writing about a character who's acting in a school play, you might use the play's acts as your time marker, and little things that went wrong as your focus. Something like this . . .

Actually making up some more writing so they can see the technique in use in yet another example.

In the first act, little Mary Stewart cried for her mother instead of saying her lines.

Notice...	Actual Text of Minilesson...
	In the second act, Billy Hollingsworth pulled the hair of one of the seven dwarfs and started a fight.
	So by the third act when Tommy's big disaster happened, everyone was ready for it . . .
Ending with an invitation for students to try some writing like this in their own work.	And then you go on writing, slowing the time down as you describe Tommy's acting disaster in detail.
	You might want to play around in your notebooks and try writing scenes that move quickly through time. Experiment a little with it and see what you come up with. Be sure and let us know if you do try this so we can study your examples alongside these others.

Sometimes it helps if we make records on chart paper or in class reference books of the content in lessons like this. We might even include the text examples if they aren't too long, or a least a reference that tells where to find the examples. This gives students a way to revisit the content of lessons if they need it in the future. Students can even add their own examples of trying things out to these records of minilessons.

Thinking It Through...

Before reading on, you might stop and think about what strikes you in the text of this lesson—especially in contrast to the lessons on process you read in Chapter Four.

Minilesson: Making Parts of a Text Work Together

This next lesson will show students one structural possibility for making the parts of a text work together. This might be one in a series of lessons on different ways to structure texts. The example text is the picture book *Spring Thaw* written by Steven Schnur (2000). The lesson will be much shorter if students are already familiar with the text and we can just talk about how it's written rather than reading the whole text as part of the minilesson. The curriculum for the lesson is this:

◆ *One way to make the parts of a text work together is to look at the same thing happening in a variety of places at the same time.*

We would be holding the book and showing students different parts as we talk about how it's written. The text of our minilesson might go like this:

Notice...	Actual Text of Minilesson...
Returning to a text we know. *Using the author's name.* *Demonstrating how the teacher reads like a writer.*	As we are thinking about different structures for texts, I wanted to go back to this book *Spring Thaw* that we read a few days ago. I think the way this text works is very interesting. As I studied it, I realized that what Steven Schnur has done is he has taken a single event, spring thaw, and moves it through time—it's starts one night and ends the next evening at sunset. But he also moves it in another way.
Here we are turning the pages of the book so students can see what we're describing. We might even reread different lines of text.	If you follow along, you realize that he just kind of roams around and looks at what's happening in different places with the thawing. You start in the trees, then move to the house with water trickling from the roof, then to the raccoon stirring in its den, then the doe, the cardinal, the wagon and horses, then snow on the roof again, then geese, then the river and lake, then lambs, then maple syrup buckets. You see how it's just following that single event all around the setting?
Naming the explicit curriculum. *Explaining the teacher's moves.*	This made me realize that one way to make the parts of a text work together is to take a single event and look at how it's happening in different places. I decided to try and do this. The event I chose is the morning of a wedding day, and I tried to move around and look at everyone getting ready for the wedding. Here's what I came up with:

The first rays of morning light slide between the curtains and coax the house out of its sleep. Eyes open, and then there is just a moment's pause when they don't realize it, and then they do: today is wedding day.

Downstairs a pot of coffee starts to brew, filling the house with wonderful smells. Everyone will be up soon, getting ready.

Outside in the garden, two morning doves coo while red birds sing. You'd think they know what day it is, they sing so happily.

Across town, two strong hands grip an icing bag and carefully pipe a last rose on a delicate cake. Sweet cake, carrot cake. The groom's favorite.

Marianne Mobley, soprano in the Baptist church choir, sings as she takes a warm shower. She's practicing, filling her tiny bathroom with Ava Maria and The Lord's Prayer.

In a field just outside of town, out past Woodrow's Gas Station and the old abandoned A&P, someone snips flowers for a bouquet. White daises, wild roses, black-eyed Susans. The bride's favorite.

more, more, more...

In a quiet bedroom, one last time, a mother goes to wake her only daughter.

I didn't draft the whole thing; I was just trying to see if I could do it. I took a single event—getting ready for the wedding—and moved it around to see how it was happening in different places.

This is a way of structuring a text you might want to try. Your event could be anything—getting ready for a big dance, Christmas Eve night, the birth of a baby sister or brother—anything. Then you try writing it so you look around at how different people or animals or things are involved in the same event. Just kind of move it around to different scenes.

Showing the curriculum in use. Helps students "untie" it from the topic of the first example.

Naming the curriculum again— tied to the example.

Helping them envision ways they might try this text structure.

Notice...	Actual Text of Minilesson...
Inviting students to try this structure in their own writing work.	You might want to look through your notebooks just to see if you have any material that might work as an event and then play around with structuring some text this way. See what you come up with. If you like it, you might use it as the start of a draft. Let us know if you try it.

Minilesson: Making the Language Work

This next minilesson could be one of a series of lessons on general crafting techniques, or a more specific series of lessons that show interesting ways to use verbs to make writing stronger. The text example comes from the last section of Gary Paulsen's *Clabbered Dirt, Sweet Grass* (1992)—yet another treasure trove of how to make the language work. The chapter book, a lyrical tribute to life on a farm, is organized into four sections, one for each season. *Winter* is the last section of the book, and after a few short paragraphs of description about winter at the beginning of the section, Paulsen writes these two sentences and makes each one its own paragraph:

> Winter grips, they say.
> Spring opens, summer lets, fall gathers, and winter grips. (106)

If all the students had not read the book, we would begin by telling them about the book—what it's about and how it works its way through the seasons. We would show them that there are a few paragraphs at the beginning of this section and summarize their contents, then show them these two specific sentences. After this introduction, we'll teach the students this:

◆ *You can use the verbs in a series of straight, subject–verb sentences to compare a number of things.*

The text of the minilesson might go like this:

Notice...	Actual Text of Minilesson...
Gary is so familiar to us as writers, we call him by his first name.	I think this sentence of Gary's is another great example of the amazing work verbs can do in our writing. I looked at it very closely and I realized that what he has done is he has written a series of straight, subject-verb sentences and connected them as one. The subjects are the seasons, and then the verbs do all the work—opens, lets, gathers, grips. They each capture a very big idea and, in a single word, they compare four distinct things: the seasons. It's like the comparison works its way across the verbs.
Naming what we've noticed happening in the text.	
Naming the curriculum explicitly.	I decided I would try it—I would try writing a series of short, straight, subject-verb sentences and let the verbs compare something. It took me awhile to think of a scene and a topic where I could do it. I needed something where the verbs could be active and very descriptive at the same time. Finally I thought of a family and how they might all respond differently to something. Here's what I came up with:
Letting them be insiders on our process of trying this.	
	While everyone in Sara's family had different ways of responding to that horrible time in their lives, each of them was consistent in his or her own way.
	Her daddy always hollered.
	Her daddy hollered, her mama wept, Michael sulked, Eddie fought, and Sara avoided.
	I guess they found comfort in being consistent.
Showing the curriculum in use. Helps students "untie" it from the topic of the first example.	It's funny because this is not actually a story I've written. I don't know who these characters are or what the horrible time was all about—I kind of want to write it to find out! Anyway, I think I pulled it off and got my verbs to work like Gary's.
Just talking to them—writer to writers.	This is something you might want to try too. You may struggle as I did to think of a scene where the verbs will

Sometimes the spontaneous examples we make up aren't so good—but that's okay. They demonstrate the "just try it" aspect of this work. Inviting them to try it.

work in this way, but it's worth a try. Like maybe you might be comparing the different sports that you play and you think of something like this . . . let's see . . . *In soccer I glide, in basketball I float, and in football I barrel across the field.* Okay, that's not so good but you get the picture. Let the verbs show the differences in something. Keep the subject-verb phrases short, and maybe even connected in the same sentence. You might play around with this in your notebooks and see what you come up with. If you like it, you can use it in the drafts where you're required to show you know how to do interesting verb work. Okay, let's get writing.

Minilesson: Making Pictures Work with Text

Let's look now at a minilesson on how to use pictures to help a writer add detail to a picture book without using more words. This would be part of a series of lessons that show all kinds of "work" the pictures can do in a text. We might

Thinking It Through...

You may find it helpful to take the content of these minilessons and try it yourself. See if you can write your own example with a different topic. Remember, we don't really own curriculum knowledge until we can envision how it would be used to write another text.

teach this lesson to very young writers who are still doing a good bit of their composing in pictures, or with more experienced writers who are specifically trying to create picture book texts.

We'll use Frank Asch's book *The Earth and I* (1994), which should be familiar to the students before the lesson. We'll show students the particular section of the book where the narrator says, "Then I listen to her." He's already told us that he and the Earth are friends and that he tells her what's on his mind and that she listens to him. After this sentence, "Then I listen to her" there is a two-page spread and another half spread that have no words on them but give you a clear picture of what the boy would be listening to—a rainstorm. We would show this part to students and then in the minilesson teach them this:

♦ *After setting up an idea with words, you can use a series of pictures to add detail to those words.*

The lesson might go something like this:

Notice...	Actual Text of Minilesson...
	See what Frank Asch is doing here? He's using these pictures to tell us part of the story. The boy tells us that he listens to the Earth, but he doesn't use words to tell us what she sounds like or what she says. He uses the pictures. We look at them and we hear the Earth. We hear the first fat raindrop plop down, and then the thunder and lightening and the many, many raindrops coming down. We hear them loud as the boy is running outside in the storm, and then softer once he's inside looking out the window at them. We hear the Earth through the pictures and we don't need words.
Talking them through what we've noticed and showing how it works in the text.	
Naming the curriculum specifically.	So what Frank Asch is doing is he uses some words to set us up for something and then lets the pictures finish the idea for us. I tried to do this too. Let me show you. This is a story about a birthday in my family. On this page you can see I have written these words:
	Hannah couldn't believe her eyes. There were presents everywhere.
We would actually create this text to show them. *Illustrate some pages that work in this way then talk them through them.*	And you can see I have Hannah's picture zoomed in really close on her face so you can see how surprised she is. Then look, as you turn the pages, I just show a present or two on each of the next four pages. A shiny bike and helmet on this one, a set of *Boxcar Children* books on this

Notice...	Actual Text of Minilesson...

	one, a new dress and shoes on this one, and an aquarium with fish on this one.
	I did what Frank Asch did. I set you up by telling you there were lots of presents, then I let my pictures show you what those presents were.
Naming the curriculum again here.	This is something any of you might try in your writing, letting your words work together like Frank and I did. If you were writing about your friend coming over, for example, you could write something like this with words:
Helping them envision trying this in their own writing.	*We had so many adventures that day.*
	You would set us up to wonder what kinds of adventures, but then in your next pages of illustrations you could show us. One picture might be of you two walking through the woods, another of you catching tadpoles in the creek. Just show us what those adventures are with the pictures.
Giving another example just to help the younger ones a little more to see different options for this technique.	Or let's say you were writing a book about school and you said:
	We have lots of supplies at school.
	And then on the next pages you showed pencils and markers, book bags and rulers and stuff. You show us the supplies.
Inviting them to try it and reminding them one more time of the need for set-up words.	So you see how this works? If you try this in your writing, be sure to set us up with some words so we know what the pictures are supposed to be. Let me know if you do try this because I'll certainly want to have a look at it.

That second example can be really critical for our youngest writers. Sometimes they have a tendency to go try, not just the technique of the lesson, but the actual example we used in the lesson. This is not a big problem because we haven't written a whole text for them as an example. But we do want to help them realize that using the technique doesn't mean you have to write about the topic of the example. We can take care of a lot of this by giving multiple examples in the lessons and by helping them in our conferences to see possibilities for the techniques in the individual work they've got going.

Showing and Telling in Lessons

In minilessons like these, the examples are so critical. The curriculum is very abstract without the examples that *show* students what these options and techniques look like in actual texts. Just look at the six curriculum statements from these four lessons by themselves and you can see how lifeless and abstract they are without the examples:

◆ *One way to move a story through time is to have a "plot anchor" that keeps you focused and helps you leave out other details.*
◆ *Markers of time and place can help you move a story forward in time quickly.*
◆ *Shorter paragraphs can help show the reader that time is moving quickly.*
◆ *One way to make the parts of a text work together is to look at the same thing happening in a variety of places at the same time.*
◆ *You can use the verbs in a series of straight, subject-verb sentences to compare a number of things.*
◆ *After setting up an idea with words, you can use a series of pictures to add detail to those words.*

When we write our own examples that show the options or techniques in use, we accomplish several things. First, we find that we understand how the writing works much better after we have tried it ourselves. We know that if we can't do it, we will have a hard time helping our students see how they can do it. We also gain a tremendous amount of "clout" with our students because we are not suggesting they try things that we have never tried ourselves. Through our examples, they come to see us as being like them in that way— writers who try things out. We don't have to worry about writing our examples well, though we will often find that we really like what we have written when we try something snappy a professional writer has shown us. That's why we're trying things after all—they should lead us to good writing.

With series of lessons like these, the goal of the teaching is not to make sure every student can successfully "do" each thing we have taught. The goal is to get a number of possibilities up in the room and expect students to experiment with them. At the end of a series of lessons on a particular aspect of writing, many teachers require students to submit a finished piece of writing that clearly shows the influence of that teaching in the work. At the end of the series of lessons on interesting ways to use verbs, for example, students would finish a piece that shows some interesting verb work they have tried. Often students also write reflective comments about the things they tried in the writing and their decision-making process for those things.

We also know that "mastery" doesn't really work as a goal for this kind of curriculum. Sometimes students try things and manage to make them work really well in their writing, and sometimes they try them and they don't work so well. Both of these are okay. In our conferences, we can often help students fine-tune the techniques they are trying on their own. We also know that we can simply accept approximations of students trying things in their writing. We accept these because we know that this is complex, sophisticated work and that our larger goal is really to teach students to read like writers, finding possibilities for their own work across their reading lives.

References

Asch, Frank. 1994. *The Earth and I.* New York: Harcourt Brace.

Paulsen, Gary. 1992. *Clabbered Dirt, Sweet Grass.* New York: Harcourt Brace Jovanovich.

Schnur, Steven. 2000. *Spring Thaw*. Illustrated by Stacey Schuett. New York: Viking.

Spinelli, Jerry. 2000. *Stargirl*. New York: Alfred A. Knopf.

Turner, Ann. 1997. *Mississippi Mud: Three Prairie Journals.* Illustrated by Robert J. Blake. New York: Harper Collins.

Letting Authors Co-Teach the Curriculum of Products

I was asked once in an interview about teaching, "What do you think your students would say about you if we asked them to tell us about you?" The first thing out of my mouth was, "They'd tell you I really love Cynthia Rylant." And I do. She and I have been co-teachers of writing now for years, and she's never let me down. I know her work by heart and I return to it again and again in my teaching to show students writing moves they can make on their own.

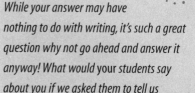

Thinking It Through...

While your answer may have nothing to do with writing, it's such a great question why not go ahead and answer it anyway! What would your students say about you if we asked them to tell us about you?

This chapter will be very short. All the chapters on the curriculum of products that have preceded this one should have made it clear that good authors are the ones to teach our students how to write well. And as we've said before, this takes so much pressure off of us as teachers of writing. We let professional authors carry the weight of writing well. We simply have to carry their weight—or the weight of their books, actually—into our classrooms and then write alongside them with our students.

Choosing Good Co-Teachers of Writing

While our ultimate goal is to end up with a whole team of authors to co-teach with us—ones we've chosen and ones *students* have chosen—it helps to start with just one. One author who will be there with us day after day in all our conferences and minilessons. One author whose work we know so well that it represents a baseline of understandings about how to write well that we carry with us in our thinking as we teach. There are a lot of applicants for these co-teaching positions in our classrooms, so how do we select?

Thinking It Through…

Who are the authors you know and love? As you read through what you need in a co-teacher of writing, ask yourself which of these authors is best suited for this position. And remember, you can love authors and not necessarily co-teach with them. It's not like you're cheating on them!

First, as a day-to-day co-teacher, we need an author who writes at least some of the kinds of things our students will be writing. While we know that the craft of writing can be generalized across genres and topics and writing for all kinds of audiences, students will need a co-teacher who can show them possibilities for whole texts as well as small moves within those texts. So, while we may have several minilessons we could teach using text examples from Barbara Kingsolver's books, we probably wouldn't choose her as a day-to-day co-teacher because most of our students aren't writing the kinds of pieces she's writing—long novels.

Next, it helps if we choose a co-teacher who has written a variety of different kinds of things—poetry, memoir, essays, different kinds of fiction—about a variety of topics. These authors help our students see a range of what's possible in a single writing life. So, while we may have several minilessons that use text examples from R. L. Stein books, we probably wouldn't choose him as a day-to-day co-teacher because there isn't a lot of variety in the kind of thing he writes.

Once our applicants have met these two criteria, then we began to look very closely at their actual writing. We ask ourselves just a few important questions. *Does this author use language and shape texts in interesting ways? Can this author carry the teaching weight of helping my students write well?* And then there is my personal favorite, *If I were stranded on a deserted island with all my students and had just this one author's work in my head, would it be enough to carry us through until we were rescued?* When we look across the author's body of work it needs to feel full with potential for our teaching.

As our list of applicants narrows, we have to think about living with this author by our side in our classroom day after day. Can we get along? Do we like this author's particular way of seeing the world? Do we like his sense of humor? Her sense of adventure? Does this feel like an author we can get to know on a first-name basis? Basically, we need to feel really connected to this author through his or her writing. Remember, we are choosing someone to *co-teach* with us, and as connected as we are to our teaching, the author we choose needs to feel right for this position.

Do we need to consider whether or not our students will feel very connected to this writer? Not necessarily. An author can show students writing moves whether the students are very connected to that author's work or not—especially when we "untie" the moves from the author's work and show students what they would look like if they tried them in their writing. Not only that, but as my friend and fellow writing teacher Isoke Nia has challenged us all to remember, students need to choose their own writing teachers from the authors *they* love and whose work *they* admire. The co-teacher we choose is just one among many teachers in the room, and it is our relationship with this author's work that will serve as an ongoing demonstration (for our students) of how to learn to write from a professional author.

Once we have selected a co-teacher, then we can spend time really getting to know this author's work. Our beginning curriculum development for

Thinking It Through... :⟳:

In the end, to choose a co-teacher you really have to just sit with a few of the author's texts and ask yourself, "What, specifically, do I see this author doing that I could teach my students how to do?" If you find a lot of answers to that question, you've probably found a good one.

products can start with text examples from just this one author. We might even do a short author study with our students where we model how to read an author's work like writers so we are left with moves we can envision making in our own writing. This author study will help us develop curriculum (because our students always notice things we don't notice) and it will show students how to learn from the authors they might choose to study on their own.

Eventually, we will want to move out and hire more co-teachers for our team. When we do, we'll look especially for authors who do particular things really well. Some of them we'll bring in for particular genres. If I am studying any type of opinion piece, for example, then Leonard Pitts, Rick Reilly, and Roger Rosenblatt are my lead co-teachers. If it's poetry, I call in Kristine O'Connell George, Nikki Grimes, William Stafford, and Jane Yolen as lead teachers. If it's the form of picture books specifically, then Donald Crews and Frank Asch are right by my side. If I just want to show students how to dance with words, sentences, and paragraphs, then Gary Paulsen, Jerry Spinelli, Jacqueline Woodson, Patricia MacLachlan, and Sandra Cisneros are right there by my teaching side.

Basically, any author who's ever done anything really well with writing can be co-teacher for a day or two or three in our classrooms. Our job is simply to read and recruit them for teaching positions. Sometimes it may be just one thing in a text that makes us think, "I have to let this author show my students how to do this." That author gets to be co-teacher for a day, or for even just a single writing conference.

Touchstone Texts

As we develop teaching relationships with authors and their work, we will find that certain texts seem to surface as very important to our teaching. These are texts that are just full of curriculum potential. We sometimes call these touchstone texts. Cynthia Rylant's two books, *Scarecrow* (1998) and *The Whales* (1996) are two of my touchstone texts. I have studied these books so much and know the writing in them so well that I have over fifty separate curriculum lessons I could teach from just these two books. As an example, Appendix E lists the more than thirty curriculum lessons I have found in *The Whales* alone.

These touchstone texts are so important to my teaching that I have literally committed each of them to memory. This isn't something that I tried to do. It just happened over time as I taught with them by my side over and over. If I really were stuck on that deserted island with all my students and none of our books made it through the shipwreck with us, I would still have Cynthia Rylant as my co-teacher because I have those two whole books in my heart and in my head.

Over time we want to develop a short stack of touchstone texts written in different genres and forms that we will get to know really well and will return to again and again in our teaching. Some of these texts will be written by our day-to-day co-teacher of writing (as *Scarecrow* and *The Whales* are for me), and some will be written by other co-teachers. A good short stack of texts like this will give us enough curriculum for a whole year of teaching. These should be texts where we have noticed a lot going on in the writing of each one. The short stack might include picture books, chapter books, editorials, feature articles, collections of poetry, speeches—any kind of writing that we think is rich with curriculum potential for our students.

In her article "Units of Study in the Writing Workshop," Isoke Nia (1999) establishes these criteria for choosing a touchstone text:

- ◆ You have read the text and you love it.
- ◆ You and your students have talked about the text a lot as readers first.
- ◆ You find many things to teach in the text.
- ◆ You can imagine talking about the text for a very long time.
- ◆ Your entire class can have access to the text.
- ◆ Your students can read the text independently or with some support.

- The text is a little more sophisticated than the writing of your best students.
- The text is written by a writer you trust.
- The text is a good example of a particular kind of writing (genre).
- The text is of the genre we are studying (if in a genre study).
- You have read the text and loved it. (6)

I love that Isoke wraps "love" around her list of other criteria. Sometimes we are tempted to choose books and other texts for our teaching because someone else loves them or thinks we should be using them. We want to guard against that. We know that if the text is really going to be a powerful force in our teaching, we have to take the need to love it seriously.

While we will obviously find curriculum for many of our minilessons from these touchstone texts, the place where they will really be helpful will be in our conferring. The teaching we do in writing conferences is on-the-spot; we can't plan ahead for it, so all we've got to go on is what we carry around in our heads. The texts we have read over and over will be the ones we'll think of first in conferences when we see students' writing and are trying to think of ways to help them raise the level of that writing. With a really good touchstone text in our heads and in our hands, we can move around a room of writers, look closely at all the different kinds of things they may be writing, and show every one of them some writing move that will raise the level of that work.

My husband's and my friend, Steve, is a huge NASCAR fan. The late Dale Earnhardt was his favorite driver, and I'll never forget the day we walked into his house and Steve was almost trembling with excitement. "I have to show you what I got," he said. And he led us into the living room and there, standing proudly next to the television set, was a life-size cardboard cutout of the late Dale Earnhardt in his racing suit.

"Is he gonna stay there?" I asked.

Suffice it to say, he has stayed there. He greets you proudly each time you walk into the room.

I often think that when I watch a really good teacher of writing, it's almost like there are life-size cardboard cutouts of authors all around the room. Jane Yolen is standing up by the chalkboard and Eloise Greenfield is just by the door to welcome students as they enter. Arnold Adoff is back by Michael's desk and Bruce Brooks is standing proudly between Tara and Steven. Jaqueline Woodson is patiently moving around the room with the teacher as she confers, standing right by each desk. With a room full of authors to help us, teaching writing doesn't have to be so lonely.

References

Nia, Isoke Titilayo. (1999). "Units of Study in the Writing Workshop." *Primary Voices K–6* (8) 1.

Rylant, Cynthia. 1996. *The Whales*. New York: Blue Sky Press.

———. 1998. *Scarecrow*. Illustrated by Lauren Stringer. New York: Harcourt Brace.

Using the Appendices

As you use the example lists in Appendices A–D, please keep the following in mind:

✓ These appendices are not meant to be comprehensive lists. What's more, the books on these lists are not *the* books you must have to teach writing, nor are the curriculum statements the *only* curriculum statements. These are simply representative examples meant to help demonstrate more of the *kinds* of things to look for in the texts in your library. Over time, you'll want to find your own curriculum and text examples and add them to these lists.

✓ As they are easier to locate than articles from newspapers and magazines, I have chosen to include only text examples from books in these lists. Most of the selected text examples are picture books (unless otherwise noted as novels). But with the exception of Appendix D (which is curriculum specific to the picture book form) *none* of the curriculum statements imply that a writer must be using the picture book form for the curriculum to make sense. Use your power of envisioning to think about how students might use the curriculum in creating other forms of texts.

✓ Unless specifically stated, all of the curriculum statements could be used to write in any genre and for any purpose. This is why the generic word *text* is used. Use your power of envisioning to think about how students might use the curriculum statements to create texts in different genres for different purposes.

✓ Remember that structural possibilities (Appendix B) may be used to make all the parts of a short text work together, or just a small part of a longer text.

✓ Some texts may be listed under more than one structural possibility (Appendix B). If this is the case, it means that the text has more than one structural device at work.

✓ Remember, none of the curriculum statements or text examples matter if they don't help us envision possibilities we can share with our student writers.

Appendix A
Just to Get a Feel for It: Ten Examples of Curriculum for General Approaches to Writing

Curriculum statement:	*A text can be written as a collection of short narrative pieces about a place, time, event, or topic. Each narrative piece can stand alone.*
Text examples:	*In My Momma's Kitchen.* 1999. Jerdine Nolen. Illus. by Colin Bootman.
	Tall Tales: Six Amazing Basketball Dreams. 2000. Charles R. Smith.

Curriculum statement:	*The narrator of a text can be an inanimate object.*
Text examples:	*Barn.* 1996. Debby Atwell.
	Cave. 2000. Diane Siebert. Illus. by Wayne McLoughlin.
	If a Bus Could Talk: The Story of Rosa Parks. 1999. Faith Ringgold.

Curriculum statement:	*A text can be written as an accompaniment to an album of photos.*
Text examples:	*Looking Back.* 1998. Lois Lowry.

Curriculum statement: *A text can be written as a series of letters.*

Text examples: *Around the World/Who's Been There?* 1999. Lindsay Barret George.

The Magpie Song. 1995. Laurence Anholt. Illus. by Dan Williams.

P.S. Longer Letter Later. 1998. Paula Danzinger and Ann M. Martin. (novel)

Curriculum statement: *A piece of writing can be introduced with a collage of quotes (on the topic of the writing) from different people.*

Text examples: *Last Licks: A Spaldeen Story.* 1999. Carrie Best. Illus. by Diane Palmisciano.

Curriculum statement: *A text can be written with a series of different narrators.*

Text examples: *Voices of the Alamo.* 2000. Sherry Garland. Illus. by Ronald Himler.

The Poisonwood Bible. 1998. Barbara Kingsolver. (novel)

Curriculum statement: *A text can be written entirely as a conversation.*

Text examples: *Momma, Where Are You From?* 2000. Marie Bradby. Illus. by Chris K. Soentpiet.

Now What Can I Do? 2001. Margaret Park. Illus. by Melissa Sweet.

One More Time, Mama. 1999. Sue Alexander. Illus. by David Soman.

Ring! Yo? 2000. Chris Raschka.

Sailing Off to Sleep. 2001. Linda Ashman. Illus. by
    Susan Winter.

Curriculum statement:	*The main body of a text (story, description, essay, etc.)* *can have facts embedded around it.*
Text examples:	*Bat Loves the Night*. 2001. Nicola Davies. Illus. by Sarah Fox-Davies.

Bat Loves the Night. 2001. Nicola Davies. Illus. by
    Sarah Fox-Davies.

Cook-a-Doodle-Doo! 1999. Janet Stevens and Susan
    Stevens Crummel. Illus. by Janet Stevens.

Gentle Giant Octopus. 1998. Karen Wallace. Illus.
    by Mike Bostock.

Sacred Places. 2000. Philemon Sturges. Illus. by
    Giles Laroche.

Supermarket. 2001. Kathleen Krull. Illus. by
    Melanie Hope Greenberg.

Curriculum statement: *A text might be a collection of poems that tells about a topic or tells a story. If the poems tell a story, they are written as a series that moves through time.*

Text examples: *All by Herself*. 1999. Ann Whitford Paul. Illus. by
    Michael Steirnagle.

Amber Was Brave, Essie Was Smart. 2001. Vera B.
    Williams.

*From the Bellybutton of the Moon/Del Ombligo de la
    Luna*. 1998. Francisco X. Alarcón. Illus. by
    Maya Christina Gonzales.

Learning to Swim. 2000. Ann Turner. (memoir)

Love That Dog. 2001. Sharon Creech. (novel)

My Man Blue. 1999. Nikki Grimes. Illus. by
    Jerome Lagarrigue.

The Other Side. 1998. Angela Johnson. (memoir)

River Friendly/River Wild. 2000. Jane Kurtz. Illus. by Neil Brennan.

Stepping Out with Grandma Mac. 2001. Nikki Grimes. Illus. by Angelo.

Voices of the Alamo. 2000. Sherry Garland. Illus. by Ronald Himler.

Curriculum statement:	*A text can communicate your message when it's written to look like a kind of text readers don't normally read for pleasure or recreation.*
Text examples:	*Everything I Know About Pirates.* 2000. Tom Lichtenheld. (written like a reference book—but obviously made up of funny bogus facts)
	The Secret Knowledge of Grown-Ups: The Second File. 2001. David Wisniewski.

Appendix B
Just to Get a Feel for It:
Examples of Curriculum for Structural Possibilities

Curriculum statement: *A text (or part of a text) can use a repeated phrase as a transitional device at the* end *of sections of text vignettes, descriptions, or ideas.*

Text examples: *Gifts*. 1997. Phyllis Limbacher Tildes.

Grandpa Never Lies. 2000. Ralph Fletcher. Illus. by Harvey Stevenson.

Making the World. 1998. Douglas Wood. Illus. by Yoshi and Hibiki Miyazaki.

Mothers Are Like That. 2000. Carol Carrick. Illus. by Paul Carrick.

My Dad. 2000. Anthony Brown.

On the Same Day in March: A Tour of the World's Weather. 2000. Marilyn Singer. Illus. by Frané Lessac.

What a Wonderful Day to Be a Cow. 1995. Carolyn Lesser. Illus. by Melissa Bay Mathis.

Curriculum statement:	*A text (or part of a text) can use a repeated phrase as a transitional device at the beginning of new sections of text vignettes, descriptions, or ideas.*
Text examples:	*A Gift from the Sea.* 2001. Kate Banks. Illus. by Georg Hallensleben.
	I Loved You Even Before You Were Born. 2001. Anne Bowen. Illus. by Greg Shed.
	This Is the Tree. 2000. Miriam Moss. Illus. by Adrienne Kennaway.
	Up North at the Cabin. 1992. Marsha Wilson Chall. Illus. by Steve Johnson.
	When I Am Old with You. 1990. Angela Johnson. Illus. by David Soman.
	When Spring Comes. 1993. Natalie Kinsey-Warnock. Illus. by Stacey Schuett.

Curriculum statement:	*A text (or part of a text) can take a single person, place, thing, or idea and describe it in different ways.*
Text examples:	*My Dad.* 2000. Anthony Brown.
	This Is the Tree. 2000. Miriam Moss. Illus. by Adrienne Kennaway.
	Uptown. 2000. Bryan Collier.
	Water. 1995. Frank Asch.

Curriculum statement:	*The ending of a text can thread back through details mentioned previously in the text.*
Text examples:	*If You Find a Rock.* 2000. Peggy Christian. Illus. by Barbara Hirsch Lember.
	If You Were Born a Kitten. 1997. Marion Dane Bauer. Illus. by JoEllen McAllister Stammen.

I Loved You Even Before You Were Born. 2001.
Anne Bowen. Illus. by Greg Shed.

Making the World. 1998. Douglas Wood. Illus. by
Yoshi and Hibiki Miyazaki.

Momma, Where Are You From? 2000. Marie
Bradby. Illus. by Chris K. Soentpiet.

Off We Go! 2000. Jane Yolen. Illus. by Laurel
Molk.

Curriculum statement:	*A text (or part of a text) can take a single idea and look at it comparatively across many different times, settings, or characters or creatures.*
Text examples:	*Animal Dads.* 1997. Sneed B. Collard III. Illus. by Steve Jenkins.

Birdsong. 1997. Audrey Wood. Illus. by Robert
Florczak.

Castles, Caves, and Honeycombs. 2001. Linda
Ashman. Illus. by Lauren Stringer.

Grandad's Prayers of the Earth. 1999. Douglas
Wood. Illus. by P.J. Lynch.

If You Were Born a Kitten. 1997. Marion Dane
Bauer. Illus. by JoEllen McAllister Stammen.

Making the World. 1998. Douglas Wood. Illus. by
Yoshi and Hibiki Miyazaki.

Market. 1996. Ted Lewin.

Throw Your Tooth on the Roof. 1998. Selby B.
Beeler. Illus. by G. Brian Karas.

When It Starts to Snow. 1998. Phillis Gershator.
Illus. by Martin Matje.

Curriculum statement: *A text (or part of a text) can be organized to follow some natural time pattern in the world—seasons, months, weeks, days, hours, minutes.*

Text examples: *Cloud Dance.* 2000. Thomas Locker.

Everett Anderson's Christmas Coming. 1991. Lucille Clifton. Illus. by Jan Spivey Gilchrist.

Grandpa Never Lies. 2000. Ralph Fletcher. Illus. by Harvey Stevenson.

January Rides the Wind. 1997. Charlotte F. Otten. Illus. by Todd L.W. Doney.

Love That Dog. 2001. Sharon Creech. (novel)

Ma Dear's Aprons. 1997. Patricia C. McKissack. Illus. by Floyd Cooper.

Mice and Beans. 2001. Pam Muñoz Ryan. Illus. by Joe Cepeda.

Night City. 1998. Monica Wellington.

Park Beat. 2001. Jonathan London. Illus. by Woodleigh Marx Hubbard.

Pieces: A Year in Poems and Quilts. 2001. Anna Grossnickle Hines.

The Web Files. 2001. Margie Palatini. Illus. by Richard Egielski.

What a Wonderful Day to Be a Cow. 1995. Carolyn Lesser. Illus. by Melissa Bay Mathis.

When the Earth Wakes. 1998. Ani Rucki.

Curriculum statement: *A text (or part of a text) can set up an idea and then simply list out examples that support the idea.*

Text examples: *Hoops.* 1997. Robert Burleigh. Illus. by Stephen T. Johnson.

Jessie's Island. 1992. Sheryl McFarlane. Illus. by
Sheena Lott.

Rumble in the Jungle. 1997. Giles Andreae. Illus.
by David Wojtowycz.

South of Haunted Dreams. 1993. Eddy L. Harris.
pp. 15–16. (novel)

Tulip Sees America. 1998. Cynthia Rylant. Illus. by
Lisa Desimini.

Curriculum statement:	*A text (or part of a text) can be organized by taking a single question and answering it several ways. Often the question is repeated several times.*
Text examples:	*Daughter, Have I Told You?* 1998. Rachel Coyne. Illus. by Virginia Halstead.

Curriculum statement:	*A text (or part of a text) can be organized to follow the natural course of something in nature—a storm, a river, the budding of a flower, etc.*
Text examples:	*River Story.* 2000. Meredith Hooper. Illus. by Bee Willey. *Storm on the Desert.* 1997. Carolyn Lesser. Illus. by Ted Rand.

Curriculum statement:	*A text (or part of a text) can be organized as a series of different questions and answers.*
Text examples:	*Do You Know What I'll Do?* 2000. Charlotte Zolotow. Illus. by Javaka Steptoe. *Have You Ever Done That?* 2001. Julie Larios. Illus. by Anne Hunter. *Momma, Where Are You From?* 2000. Marie Bradby. Illus. by Chris K. Soentpiet.

One More Time, Mama. 1999. Sue Alexander. Illus. by David Soman.

When Artie Was Little. 1996. Harriet Berg Schwartz. Illus. by Thomas B. Allen. (actually has answers and then questions)

Winter Lullaby. 1998. Barbara Seuling. Illus. by Greg Newbold.

Appendix C
Just to Get a Feel for It: Twenty Examples of Curriculum for Making the Language Work

Curriculum statement: *As a unifying element, a particular part of speech can be repeated across several sentences.* (When noticing these with students, be sure to name the part of speech that is repeated.)

Text examples:

"So I watch it, as summer fades to fall. Watch it, as me and Grandma begin to pack away our summer clothes and take down our sweaters. And start a doll-bed quilt. And finish it. I watch the world as the days grow shorter. Watch it as harvest comes . . ."

> From *Sweet, Sweet Memory*. 2000. Jacqueline Woodson. Illus. by Floyd Cooper.

". . . people come to market. They come barefoot and bent with backbreaking loads, walking for days over lonely mountain passes. They come on jungle trails and roads jammed with traffic. They come by dugout canoe from upriver or by trawler after weeks away at sea. They come any way they can."

> From *Market!* 1996. Ted Lewin.

Curriculum statement: *When a pair of words or phrases serve one function in a sentence, they don't have to be joined by a conjunction. There are other options.*

Text examples:

"Rivulets become cascades, become torrents. Washes, arroyos, canyons fill up, spill over."

From *Storm on the Desert*. 1997. Carolyn Lesser. Illus. by Ted Rand.

"The never-stop back and forth flow, like tides going in, going out."

From *Hoops*. 1997. Robert Burleigh. Illus. by Stephen T. Johnson.

"I could see it by the hand across his forehead, his troubled eyes." p. 21

From *The Islander*. 1998. Cynthia Rylant.

Curriculum statement: *For a slow, winding effect, several sentences can be combined into one.* (When studying sentences like these, it helps to name the separate sentences that have been combined. Listen to how they sound written separately.)

Text examples:

"We always stop at Toliver's barn to pull down wicked icicle swords, each one filled with sharp, clear light, and challenge each other to a sword fight." p. 15

From *Grandpa Never Lies*. 2000. Ralph Fletcher. Illus. by Harvey Stevenson.

"Mr. Zuckerman took fine care of Wilbur all the rest of his days, and the pig was often visited by friends and admirers, for nobody ever forgot the year of his triumph and the miracle of the web." p. 183

From *Charlotte's Web*. 1952. E. B. White.

Curriculum statement: *A simile is made striking when the two things compared are very, very different—except for one quality they share (which drives the simile).*

Text examples:

"Then [a Wolf eel] sinks like a nightmare deep into his den."
From *Gentle Giant Octopus*. 1998. Karen Wallace. Illus. by Mike Bostock.

Curriculum statement: *Known words can be combined in new ways to make new, just right words or phrases.* (When noticing these with students, be sure to name the part of speech of the new, combined word.)

Text examples:

"Then, fingers pocket-fumbling, Chloe searched for the food colouring."
From *Snow Story*. 1997. Nancy Hundal. Illus. by Kasia Charko.

"I am that morning-washing, bean-snapping, wagon-watching, tree-swinging, Miss Mary-waving, brown bus-riding, clothes-sprinkling, croaker-eating, Red light-playing, finger-popping, star-dreaming girl."
From *Momma, Where Are You From?* 2000. Marie Bradby. Illus. by Chris K. Soentpiet.

Curriculum statement: *Items in a series may be punctuated in a number of ways.* (When studying these, it's helpful to experiment with other ways the author might have punctuated them. Listen to differences in sound.)

Text examples:

"Koi in the pond rise to the dimpling rain, searching for something, a lotus petal, a seed, an insect."
From *Making the World*. 1998. Douglas Wood. Illus. by Yoshi and Hibiki Miyazaki.

"The river grows wider, and deeper, and stronger."
  From *River Story*. 2000. Meredith Hooper. Illus. by Bee Willey.

"At school they say I'm wired bad, or wired mad, or wired sad, or wired glad, depending on my mood and what teacher has ended up with me. But there is no doubt about it, I'm *wired*." p. 3
  From *Joey Pigza Swallowed the Key*. 1998. Jack Gantos.

"It [the barn] smelled of grain and of harness dressing and of axle grease and of rubber boots and of new rope. And whenever the cat was given a fish-head to eat, the barn would smell of fish."
  From *Charlotte's Web*. 1952. E. B. White.

Curriculum statement:	*In a list of items in a series, one way to show them all running together is to let the punctuation (commas) trail off at the end of the list. Just let the words "bump" together.*

Text examples:

". . . had always once been something else but now it was this, a place for this meeting, this great and raw alive romping, drinking, laughing, puking, crying stomping loving hating wondrous wondrous bastard of a summer dance." p. 36

". . . there is a hole and it's filled with sunfish, crappies, bream, rock bass bull-heads catfish bluegills." p. 53

"By the fourth sack, fifth sack, tenth sack fifteenth sack twentieth sack there is no more counting, only the work." p. 82
  All from *Clabbered Dirt, Sweet Grass*. 1992. Gary Paulsen. Illus. by Ruth Wright Paulsen.

Curriculum statement: *Adjectives can come after a noun, clarifying it.*

Text examples:

"I am from beans—green, lima, and pea—picked, string, snapped, and shelled into pans . . ."

  From *Momma, Where Are You From?* 2000. Marie Bradby. Illus. by Chris
    K. Soentpiet.

Curriculum statement: *A series of sentences can work together to make each one complete. The subjects and verbs are understood from the text around them.* (When studying sentences like these, it helps to name the understood parts of each sentence.)

Text examples:

"And then she felt it. Softly at first. A gentle thumping. Then stronger. A resounding thud, thud, thud against her body." p. 2

  From *Esperanza Rising.* 2000. Pam Muñoz Ryan.

"When there are storms, Papa will stretch a rope from the door to the barn so we will not be lost when we feed the sheep and the cows and Jack and Old Bess. And Sarah's chickens, if they aren't living in the house. There will be Sarah's sea, blue and gray and green, hanging on the wall. And songs, old ones and new. And Seal with yellow eyes. And there will be Sarah, plain and tall." p. 58

  From *Sarah, Plain and Tall.* 1985. Patricia MacLachlan.

Curriculum statement: *Sometimes additions can be made to the ending idea in a sentence by simply adding details and punctuating them as separate sentences. The subjects and verbs are understood.*

Text examples:

"I thought about reading you bedtime stories. Dream Stories. Close-your-eyes stories."

> From *I Loved You Even Before You Were Born.* 2001. Anne Bowen. Illus. by Greg Shed.

"I could only stare at Ruth May's bare left shoulder, where two red puncture wounds stood out like red beads on her flesh. Two dots an inch apart, as small and tidy as punctuation marks at the end of a sentence none of us could read." p. 364

> From *The Poisonwood Bible.* 1998. Barbara Kingsolver.

"And I have to admit, he stunk. Bad." p. 14

> From *Because of Winn Dixie.* 2000. Kate DiCamillo.

Curriculum statement: *Italics can be used to punctuate direct quotes, or to punctuate direct quotes that are somehow different from regular speaking in a text.*

Text examples:

In two of Jacqueline Woodson's texts italics are used to punctuate direct quotes (as others remember them) from characters who are no longer living (literally or figuratively). Direct quotes from living characters are punctuated with the more common quotation marks.

Like nothing, Charlie said. *I don't feel like nothing anymore.* p. 58

> From *Miracle's Boys.* 2000. Jacqueline Woodson.

The earth changes, Grandpa said, as he planted his garden.

> From *Sweet, Sweet Memory.* 2000. Jacqueline Woodson.

Curriculum statement: *A paragraph can be a single word or phrase or sentence. Often it sets up what is to follow it in the next paragraph.*

Text examples:

"Uncle Jack's words.

That's all I know of him. His letters and the words he's lent to us to be a part of him." p. 21

From *Heaven*. 1998. Angela Johnson.

"And here it comes.

A thin rim of orange-red, so deep and strong my heart almost breaks with the fierceness of that color. Moment by moment, there is more of it to see. So hot and bright, I cannot look but at the edges. Even when I look away, look clear away to the waning edge of darkness, I can see that color in my mind's eye, feel it beating in my very blood. I breathe color." pp. 2–3

From *Getting Near to Baby*. 1999. Audrey Couloumbis.

Curriculum statement: *Two sentences can sort of collapse together when the subject and verb of the second are clearly understood from the first: i.e., "I hold my breath, (I am) waiting."*

Text examples:

"I hold my breath, waiting."

From *Come On, Rain!* 1999. Karen Hesse. Illus. by Jon J. Muth.

"My eyes fly open and I catch my breath, scared."

From *Beekeepers*. 1998. Linda Oatman High. Illus. by Doug Chayka.

"The sun slips out, winter pale."

From *On the Same Day in March*. 2000. Marilyn Singer. Illus. by Frané Lessac.

Curriculum statement: *A word can be immediately repeated in a text for effect.*

Text examples:

"Sometimes by day an owl goes floating away, away to where wheat and sky are one."

From *The Barn Owls*. 2000. Tony Johnston. Illus. by Deborah Kogan Ray.

Curriculum statement: *One way to make language fresh is to use a word in a surprising way, a way readers don't expect it to be used.*

Text examples:

". . . then chasing after the iceman's wagon, tiny winter on wheels, begging for chips of shaved ice."

From *Summerbath, Winterbath*. 2001. Eileen Spinelli. Illus. by Elsa Warnick.

"In the forests of northern California branches of giant sequoias reach up to rock the moon and cradle the Western sky . . ."

From *Across America, I Love You*. 2000. Christine Loomis. Illus. by Kate Kiesler.

Curriculum statement: *A sentence can have layers of words functioning as objects of a single verb or single preposition. The layers communicate several possibilities or comparisons.*

Text examples:

"She will be bundled in a
     bark cloth blanket
          knitted bunting
    kaross cape
    and hugged into belonging."

From *She Is Born*. 1999. Virginia Kroll. Illus. by John Rowe. Spaces shown because they serve like marks of punctuation.

"... until finally someone breaks an arm leg wrist ankle nose, cuts a fore-head or cheek and runs to the house and the sliding is stopped." p. 111

From *Clabbered Dirt, Sweet Grass*. 1992. Gary Paulsen. Illus. by Ruth Wright Paulsen.

Curriculum statement:	*A series of short sentences, constructed alike, has rhythm—especially when the last one has the most syllables.*

Text examples:

"Her beady eyes open. Her pixie ears twitch. She shakes her thistledown fur."

From *Bat Loves the Night*. 2001. Nicola Davies. Illus. by Sarah Fox-Davies.

Curriculum statement:	*Sometimes sentences work like items in a series—they form a list of elements that go together. When this is the case, the last one in the list can effectively start with and.*

Text examples:

"In November, at winter's gate, the stars are brittle. The sun is a sometime friend. And the world has tucked her children in, with a kiss on their heads, till spring."

From *In November*. 2000. Cynthia Rylant. Illus. by Jill Kastner.

"For I knew that the creatures that lay all around me were as real and mortal as I. I understood their frail bodies, their small beating hearts suddenly silenced. And I knew, somehow, that she was not one of them." pp. 41–42

From *The Islander*. 1998. Cynthia Rylant.

Curriculum statement:	*One way to communicate that someone is simply go-ing through the motions is to write a series of short,*

simple sentences that all begin with a subject and action verb (the motions!).

Text examples:

"I lurked in the shadows for the rest of the day. I went straight home after school. I stayed in my room. I came out only for dinner. I told my parents I had a project to do. I paced. I lay on my bed and stared at the ceiling. I stared out the window. I laid the card on my study desk. I picked it up. I read it. I read it. I read it. I played "Hi, Leo" over and over in my head. I tossed darts at the corkboard on the back of my door . . ." p. 74

  From *Stargirl*. 2000. Jerry Spinelli.

Curriculum statement: *Strong nouns and verbs can do much of the descriptive work in a text.*

Text examples:

"Under the sandy shuffle of the surf, he could hear the clack of the crab's shielded backs bumping and scraping together."

  From *Crab Moon*. 2000. Ruth Horowitz. Illus. by Kate Kiesler.

Appendix D
Just to Get a Feel for It: Ten Examples of Curriculum Specific to Picture Books

Note: Only one text example is listed for each of these. Many of these specifics of picture book curriculum are quite common in texts, and so examples are very easy to find.

Curriculum statement:	*Words can be placed anywhere on the pages in relation to the illustrations. Sometimes they are consistent throughout a book, sometimes they vary from spread to spread.*
Text example:	*Dumpy La Rue.* 2001. Elizabeth Winthrop. Illus. by Betsy Lewin.
Curriculum statement:	*Illustrations can be used to indicate who is speaking the words on a page.*
Text example:	*Ring! Yo?* 2000. Chris Rashka.
Curriculum statement:	*Illustrations can be rendered so that we see things the way a particular narrator would see them. For example, everything from ground level if an ant is telling the story.*

Text example:	*Loki & Alex.* 2001. Charles R. Smith. The pictures are in black and white when the dog narrates and in color when the boy narrates.
Curriculum statement:	*A picture book can have insets of information embedded in the illustrations—in addition to the running text. This information may wrap around the illustration or be boxed off in some way.*
Text example:	*My First Garden.* 2000. Tomek Bogacki. (wrapped around pictures) *Supermarket.* 2001. Kathleen Krull. Illus. by Melanie Hope Greenberg. (boxed off)
Curriculum statement:	*An illustration can actually continue over from one two-page spread to the next two-page spread.*
Text example:	*Sail Away.* 1995. Donald Crews.
Curriculum statement:	*Illustrations can have an illustrated border around them. Usually the content of the border illustration is connected somehow to the text and the illustration within the border.*
Text example:	*The Wonderful Happens.* 2000. Cynthia Rylant. Illus. by Coco Dowley.
Curriculum statement:	*At the beginning or end of a picture book, there can be a section of straight prose facts that relate to the topic of the picture book. Often these read like little encyclopedia entries.*

Text example:	*Crab Moon.* 2000. Ruth Horowitz. Illus. by Kate Kiesler.

Curriculum statement:	*The print in a picture book can be manipulated to make meaning—changes in color, size, font and the left-to-right paths are the most common manipulations.*

Text example:	*When Papa Snores.* 2000. Melinda Long. Illus. by Holly Meade.

Curriculum statement:	*Running text can be continued from one two-page spread to the next—in other words, for illustration purposes a single sentence may continue across several spreads. Sometimes an ellipsis is used to hold the reading to the next page, sometimes it's not.*

Text example:	*Canoe Days.* 1999. Gary Paulsen. Pictures by Ruth White Paulsen.

Curriculum statement:	*Changing the color of the background of illustrations can communicate a change of meaning or help organize a text.*

Text example:	*So Far from the Sea.* 1998. Eve Bunting. Illus. by Chris K. Soentpiet.

Appendix E
What I Know About Writing from Knowing
The Whales, by Heart

Cynthia Rylant's lyrical tribute to these beautiful creatures reads like a song. Because the text is so wonderfully crafted, it contains a plethora of things to know about how to write well. This single touchstone text has taught me so much about writing. It's taught me:

- ◆ *A text can simply describe something in layers of details.*
- ◆ *One way to open and close a piece like this is to use present-progressive verbs in the lead and the ending, and present tense verbs in the layers of details in the middle.*
- ◆ *You may use part of the proper name of something to describe it.*
- ◆ *One way to make a verb striking is to choose an action we don't usually think of as something the subject would do.*
- ◆ *Two separate sentences may share the same subject (it's stated in the first one, understood in the second).*
- ◆ *A colon may be used to set up a list.*
- ◆ *A list of things in a sentence (items in a series) may be connected with only commas (no and between them).*
- ◆ *The last item in a list of things in a sentence (items in a series) may be separated and punctuated as its own sentence.*

◆ When listing items in a series, you may give the list rhythm by making the last item have the most syllables (demonstrated three times in the text).

◆ You may create a play on words by using some literal meaning of a proper noun in conjunction with the proper noun.

◆ One way to create rhythm is to repeat a sentence construction a few times in a row.

◆ Items in a series may actually be whole sentences in a series. If you have sentences in a series, you may begin the last one with and—much as you would the last item in a series within a sentence.

◆ Personification is generally achieved through specific verb and noun choices.

◆ A list of things in a sentence (items in a series) may be connected with and between each item and no commas.

◆ One way to create rhythm is to repeat parts of phrases in a series of phrases in a single sentence (demonstrated twice in the text).

◆ Ellipses may be used to mark a pause in the text.

◆ Several phrases set apart by commas may slow a sentence down.

◆ The subject and verb of a declarative sentence may be understood from the surrounding text and not stated in the sentence.

◆ A simile is made striking when the two things compared are very, very different—except for one quality they share (which drives the simile).

◆ You may connect two verb phrases in a single sentence with a comma and no conjunction.

◆ Proper nouns may lend a credible specificity to writing.

◆ A list of things (items in a series) may be punctuated as separate sentences with the subject and verb of the list stated only in the opening sentence.

◆ Sometimes a list (items in a series) may be written in pairs—two items connected by and—separated from other pairs by a mark of punctuation.

◆ An emphatic sentence may stand with no subject or verb if it is made complete by the text that surrounds it.

- *Ellipses may be used for a sentence that trails off and doesn't end, indicating the narrator cannot find the words to finish it.*
- *A sentence may begin with the conjunction* and *at some shifting point in the text, often indicating a point where many things will come together.*
- *When a sentence ends with a verb or verb phrase, you may start a new sentence with that same verb (and no subject) and add a little more detail to it.*
- *One way to end a piece is to come back again to details that were used earlier in the text.*
- *Two prepositional phrases may be joined with just a comma and no conjunction.*
- *You may use a common noun in a new way—to name something it doesn't normally name.*
- *You may use an indefinite article* (a) *when then reader expects a definite article* (the).

We often wonder, does a writer like Cynthia Rylant think about language in this way (as it's pulled apart here) when she's crafting a text like this? No, I'm almost sure she doesn't. A writer's knowledge of language and text and genre is implicit in the drafting process. In revision, this knowledge often becomes explicit as writers work with the fullness of what they know about language to make a text work well. As teachers of writing, however, we need to know about language and text and genre in explicit ways. The more explicit our knowledge base, the stronger our sense of writing curriculum will be and the more informed our teaching of writing.

Appendix F
Sources for Essays, Feature Articles, Editorials, and Book Reviews

Most major newspapers and magazines now have websites with both current issues and archives of past issues available. Great examples of essays, feature articles, editorials, and book reviews are now easily available from these sources. Simply search for the name of a newspaper or magazine and see what's available that might support your teaching of writing. Here are a few magazine websites for collecting examples of good writing:

Time	*www.time.com*
Time for Kids	*www.timeforkids.com*
Newsweek	*www.msnbc.com*
Teen Newsweek	*www.msnbc.com/news/nw-teennewsweek*
National Geographic	*www.nationalgeographic.com*
National Geographic World	*www.nationalgeographic.com/world*
National Geographic for Kids	*www.nationalgeographic.com/ngforkids*
Rolling Stone	*www.rollingstone.com*
Sports Illustrated	*www.cnnsi.com*
Sports Illustrated for Kids	*www.sikids.com*
Popular Science	*www.popsci.com*

And a very short list of collections of essays and feature articles with really good writing in them:

Reynolds Price's *Feasting the Heart* (2001)
Anna Quindlen's *Thinking Out Loud* (2001) and *Living Out Loud* (1992)
Rick Reilly's *The Life of Reilly* (2000)
Gary Smith's *Beyond the Game* (2001)

Index